TWAYNE'S WORLD AUTHORS SERIES

A Survey of the World's Literature

Sylvia E. Bowman, Indiana University

GENERAL EDITOR

Australia

Joseph Jones, University of Texas

EDITOR

Bernard O'Dowd

(*TWAS 36*)

TWAYNE'S WORLD AUTHORS SERIES (TWAS)

The purpose of TWAS is to survey the major writers —novelists, dramatists, historians, poets, philosophers, and critics—of the nations of the world. Among the national literatures covered are those of Australia, Canada, China, Eastern Europe, France, Germany, Greece, India, Italy, Japan, Latin America, New Zealand, Poland, Russia, Scandinavia, Spain, and the African nations, as well as Hebrew, Yiddish, and Latin Classical literatures. This survey is complemented by Twayne's United States Authors Series and English Authors Series

The intent of each volume in these series is to present a critical-analytical study of the works of the writer; to include biographical and historical material that may be necessary for understanding, appreciation, and critical appraisal of the writer; and to present all material in clear, concise English—but not to vitiate the scholarly content of the work by doing so.

Bernard O'Dowd

By HUGH ANDERSON

Twayne Publishers, Inc. :: New York

For

Dr. E. Morris Miller

Prince of Australian Bibliographers

Preface

WRITING in tribute to Bernard O'Dowd shortly after his death in 1953 at the age of eighty-seven years, Nettie Palmer, herself a respected contributor to Australian letters, attempted to define what his poetry had meant to her generation in the early years of this century. "It is hard to suggest what an inspiring figure Bernard O'Dowd was in those days," she wrote, "not only to young people trying to write but to all who had urgent hopes of a better future for mankind. O'Dowd really believed in this future or 'millennia,' in spite of the scepticism suggested by his favourite punctuation mark, the note of interrogation. And for all his democratic homeliness, his generous simplicity, he had a touch of personal magic that kindled the imagination and made it easy to believe that he was not only a poet but a sage."

Throughout his career there were influential critics who denied him both titles, and since his death and the loss of the force of the attractive personality that gave such an aura to his work, another generation has grown up that can know and judge his value only from his writing. To most of these readers his poetry is puzzling, even difficult to understand fully, and the outlook almost antediluvian. It is therefore presently neglected.

O'Dowd not only gave lasting expression to Australia's national spirit and dealt confidently with her scene and history, but he was also a maker of traditions; he was a pioneer in her social and literary history; he was prominent in the country's intellectual life, in the creation of her literature, even in her law-making. Bernard O'Dowd was Australia's "poet of the dawn." Steeped in the religious, mystical, philosophical and sociological enthusiasms of the latter years of the nineteenth century, he turned this intellectual ferment to a new use, made his visions a national heritage and became for some considerable time, the leading spokesman of the age.

With a literary reach of seventy-five years, O'Dowd spans the wide gulf in Australian literature between the racy bush ballad of the nineties and the modernism of the twenties. In many ways he anticipated the better aspects of both movements by as much as twenty years. His idiosyncratic poetry is itself a curious blend of simple verse form and erudite thought, of democratic and patriotic fervors, of the traditional and the contemporary.

O'Dowd must be taken account of, for he has something worthwhile to say, even if he decimates the dictionary to do so. His work remains valuable in the present day and is not merely an historical landmark. While any new generation coming to O'Dowd's verse will be, as R. G. Howarth said in 1953, "impressed by its sincerity, its thoughtfulness, and the extraordinary learning of the poet," they will also re-discover Australia's first poet who wrote a poetry of ideas. They will find abundant striking thoughts, and a far-ranging imagination; they will find poetry that is brilliant in phrase, intellect and passion.

A scrap of paper found among his literary remains is probably as good a summation of his life as could be found:

Literarum Gloriam Sitii, Videt Dei.

O'Dowd's own translation was, "He sought the glory of literature, he sees the glory of God."

For permission to quote substantially from the collected edition of Bernard O'Dowd's *Poems*, including the introduction to that volume by Walter Murdoch, I am indebted to the Lothian Publishing Co. Pty. Ltd.

Messrs. Angus and Robertson Ltd. agreed to quotations from A. A. Phillips' introduction to the selected poems of O'Dowd and from *Australian Literary Essays* by Frederick T. Macartney.

Numerous extracts from Victor Kennedy and Nettie Palmer's biography of the poet are used by kind permission of Melbourne University Press. I wish also to thank Professor T. Inglis Moore of the Australian National University for permission to quote from his *Six Australian Poets*.

Considerable use of manuscripts in the Mitchell Library, Sydney, and the National Library of Australia, Canberra, was made with the permission of their respective Librarians. The development of the views expressed in this book owes much to the encouragement of Professor E. Morris Miller, and more so to Bernard O'Dowd himself for access to his manuscripts and papers and for stimulating expositions of his views on life and literature.

Contents

Preface

Chronology

1.	The Boy From the Bush	15
2.	Words From the Master	23
3.	The Burning Bush	29
4.	Poet and Politician	38
5.	Democracy and Conscience	47
6.	Questions Without Answers	55
7.	The Ships of Love	66
8.	Slave of the Striking Word	73
9.	Poetry Militant	82
10.	The Intriguing Balance	90
11.	Sybil and Siren	99
12.	For Love Alone	111

Notes and References 122

Selected Bibliography 129

Index 135

Chronology

1866   Born at Beaufort, Victoria, Australia, eldest son of Bernard and Anne O'Dowd, née Mulholland.

1876   Moved to Ballarat, where he attended Mount Pleasant elementary school.

1880   Won State Exhibition.

1881   Student at Grenville College, Ballarat.

1882   First poem printed in Ballarat *Evening Post.*

1883   Head Teacher, Saint Alipius' school for boys until discharged for heresy. Opened Beaufort College as a private school.

1885   Passed Public Service entrance examination.

1886   Moved to Melbourne to take up a position as clerk in the Crown Solicitor's Office. Joined the Melbourne Progressive Lyceum.

1887   Assistant-librarian, Supreme Court Library.

1888   Editor of the *Lyceum Tutor.*

1889   Graduated B.A., University of Melbourne. Married Evangeline Fryer.

1890   Began correspondence with Walt Whitman.

1894   First poem printed in the Sydney *Bulletin.*

1897   Joint editor of the *Tocsin,* and contributor of verses and weekly column of prose.

1901   Personal crisis; love-affair and return to Catholicism.

1902   *Democracy and Conscience* delivered as a lecture to the Melbourne Lyceum and published separately.

1903   First book of poetry, *Dawnward?*, published.

1906   Publication of *The Silent Land.*

1907   *Dominions of the Boundary* published. Contributor of weekly literary column, and verse, to the *Socialist.*

1909   Estranged from wife; love-affair with Mrs. Marie Pitt. *The Seven Deadly Sins* published. *Poetry Militant* delivered at the Annual Meeting of the Australian Literature Society and published as a pamphlet.

1912   Publication of *The Bush.*

1913 Appointed Assistant Parliamentary Draughtsman for the State of Victoria.

1919 Deserted his wife to live with Marie Pitt.

1921 *Alma Venus!* published.

1931 Appointed Chief Parliamentary Draughtsman for Victoria.

1934 Declined to accept a knighthood for his services to Literature.

1935 Retired from the Public Service.

1941 Publication of a collected edition of *Poems*.

1942 A small volume of prose, *Fantasies,* published.

1948 Death of Marie Pitt.

1953 Death of Bernard O'Dowd.

CHAPTER ONE

The Boy From the Bush

BERNARD Patrick O'Dowd arrived in the city of Melbourne at the beginning of 1886 to take up a position as a clerk in the office of the Crown Solicitor for the State of Victoria. This gangling, ginger-haired youth from the country was met at the railway station by two boyhood friends, Fred Woods and Harry de Baere, and taken to a cheap boarding house in a nearby suburb. His work for some time was copying depositions in criminal jurisdiction and civil law conveyancing, until seconded to the Supreme Court library as an assistant. After hours, in contrast to the round of rather commonplace activity of finding and replacing legal documents, O'Dowd was involved in organizations devoted to liberal thought.

The eldest son of Irish immigrants, Bernard was born at Beaufort in April 1866 where his father was a police constable. His parents were sincere and devout Catholics who nourished their son's mind with a strange mixture of myth and legend, piety and family traditions, that mingled naturally together. Many years later in *The Bush* he described this background:

> Once while my mother by a spreading tree
> Our church's sober rubric bade me con,
> My vagrant eyes among the boughs would see
> Forbidden wings and wizard aprons on
> Father's "wee people" from their Irish glades
> Brighten and darken with your lights and shades
> And I would only read again those stern leaves
> For whispered bribe that, when their tale I told,
> We would go and look for fairies in the fern-leaves
> And red-capped leprechauns with crocks of gold.

His schooling began quite early and continued in a number of the new non-denominational State Schools devoted to instruction that was supposedly free, compulsory, and secular. The boy showed a bent for study and read omnivorously; *Paradise Lost* at eight, Hume at nine, and Virgil at ten years of age. At the same time, he was an acolyte, chanting responses at the Mass, on Sundays.

When his parents moved to the solid, prosperous city of Ballarat in 1876 they were faced with the choice of keeping Bernard at a State School or sending him to a Catholic college. As they hoped he would obtain an Exhibition entitling him to six years secondary education, and not then open to church schools, they went against their religious convictions and enrolled the boy at Mount Pleasant in Ballarat East. In 1880, O'Dowd was a successful candidate for this particular scholarship and took on further study at Grenville College. Under the conditions of the examination he also matriculated to the University of Melbourne and was able to sit for his Arts degree subjects in Ballarat. As evidence of his encyclopaedic mind, while attending the College during the day, he studied mathematics and surveying at night classes at the Ballarat School of Mines and Industries on a second scholarship that he had won while still an elementary school pupil.

One of his fellow students at the School of Mines was Bill Allen, whose father owned the local *Evening Post* newspaper. Allen invited Bernard to contribute some of the verses he had been shown to the "Poet's Corner." During the first half of 1882, O'Dowd had six poems printed in the *Evening Post* under such titles as "O Leave Her," "Solitude," "To All Eternity," "My Own Dear Love," and finally, "False Accusations." His biographers consider "they were such as might be expected of a gifted boy of sixteen whose inner life was a constant ferment, but whose whole mind reverberated with the cadences of others: they dealt with tragic separations, the joys of solitude, unrequited love and hopes of happiness beyond the tomb. There was nothing in theme or treatment to mark them out from any other poet's juvenilia, but at least they gave him some practice in mastering an instrument that was to be his main means of expression."[1]

I. *A Bush Heretic*

Misfortune came upon the O'Dowd family when Bernard had completed half of his six years' scholarship. His father was permanently injured in the course of his police duties; he resigned and returned to a small farm at Beaufort. Forced to earn his living, Bernard took over the headmastership of St. Alipius' Catholic School for boys. He was then seventeen years of age and already far removed from the fundamental beliefs of his faith. Knowledge of his activities soon reached the Church authorities; the open expression of agnostic views and attendance at secularist meetings in Ballarat could not be tolerated and he was quietly replaced.

Some time afterwards, O'Dowd moved back to Beaufort and opened his own school in his mother's house. The venture prospered for a while and old friendships with Fred Woods and Harry de Baere were resumed. A mutual interest in Free Thought and the views of such men as Huxley, Lyell, and Tom Paine, took much of their spare time. Although a convinced secularist, O'Dowd flirted with the spiritualist movement and took out a subscription for the *Harbinger of Light,* the official organ of the Melbourne society. In general, he was opposed to orthodox ways of thinking, without holding fast to any particular doctrine. He was known as the iconoclast of Beaufort; an agent for the *Liberator,* the journal of the secularist organization; a participator in "Anti-God" meetings. Rumors that O'Dowd was poisoning his pupils' minds multiplied until they destroyed his school.

O'Dowd was also attempting to write poetry. On one of his regular trips to Ballarat to lecture and debate at the secular meetings, he met Tom Bury, a journalist who contributed to the Ballarat *Courier* under the name of "Tom Touchstone." Bury persuaded the young schoolteacher to try his verses in the Saturday literary page of the newspaper. The verses printed lack individual style and idiom as might be expected in a young man. Most deal with love and religion in a rather pathetic manner, but one written in May 1885 strikes a different note:

> Hark now the joy bells all around us are pealing,
> The wounds of this dark superstition are healing:
> The armies of Reason their flags are unfurling.
> And idols of Falsehood to darkness are hurling:
> And swift to the vanguard Truth's white steeds are bounding,
> While Equity's trumpets loud charges are sounding,
> And o'er the great host with golden light streaming,
> The sunform of Hope in the heavens is gleaming.

Several of the poems of this period concern a romantic verse-correspondence with Minnie Miller, another young schoolteacher who wrote as "Wattle-blossom." O'Dowd's favorite nom-de-plume was "Minnesinger," that is, a minor poet as distinguished from a Meister-singer. In a rather lengthy set of verses, dated on the manuscript 24 and 25 February 1886, O'Dowd tells the tale of love in a bush glade:

> One summer morn with sketching book in hand,
>   I took my way into the forest deep.
> The brook scarce hummed upon its silver sand,
>   And all the winds and trees had gone to sleep.
> A lovely yellow light embraced all things,
>   The wattles breathed their sighs with scented breath,
> At times was heard a passing sweep of wings,
>   All else was calm and silent still as death.

Walking "beside the bank of that sweet singing creek" he heard the sound of "angelic singing," and following it with "eager ears," came upon a "form of mould divine" resting "in a peaceful arbour on the hill." Obtaining consent of the coy maiden, the poet flashes his sketch book and draws her, passion flowing in every stroke.

A few months later, all passion spent, he cries aloud:

> I loved you long, I loved you well
>   And now, you do deceive me:
> I joy to hear the welcome bell
>   That tells me you will leave me.
> I loved you with my heart, my soul,
>   I loved you 'gainst my reason
> Kind angels held 'fore me this scroll
>   "Her love is only treason."

II. *Marching on to Hell*

Remembering those youthful days, O'Dowd said, "I had lost my bearings as far as the Church was concerned. It could do nothing for me. At the same time I was without guidance just when any sort of plausible argument might have appealed to me. I wanted to feel more sure. I wanted something that could, of its own merit, hold my confidence. The tradition and learning behind the set books of the University seemed to promise that. So I decided to go back to the University."[2] It is difficult not to surmise other, deeper, reasons behind a decision to leave the world of human problems for one of books, but there is little real evidence that such existed. He did refer, in what was little more than a hint, to a shattering emotional experience "before the age of twenty" that caused him to think he would never seek "a mate of [his] own tribe." This, however, certainly had nothing to do with losing his religious faith:

> Woe-weary my heart is, forbidding the world,
> I struggle with sickness, I writhe with despair,
> My soul from the watch-cliffs of promise is hurled,
> And gall-barbed doubtings my consciousness tear.
> O Science! you fail me; Philosophy! you:
> I find no consoling in logic, in lore.
> Wild anguishes haunt me I fly, they pursue,
> O give me, O give me a God, I implore!

The stanza quoted is a somewhat matured version of his feelings, written after he had been almost two years in Melbourne, but while still fresh from Beaufort he tended to a devil-may-care attitude in verses complete with chorus:

> The Christian God's a monster, boys,
>   His deeds proclaim him brute.
> The devil is a gentleman,
>   He gave us knowledge fruit.
> Down with the tyrant, down with the Lord,
> Down with the wielder of Oppression's rod,
> Down with the fiend-god, the vampire abhorred
> Down with Jehovah, down with God!

After such "down with" punches the chorus is quite jaunty:

> Marching on to hell, boys,
> We sing our joyful song
> With the devil as our leader, lads,
> We gaily march along.
> We'd sooner go to hell, boys,
> Than cringe beneath the rod
> As those must do who would be true
>   To heaven's demon god.

III. *Shining Banners Bright*

The young fellow who arrived in Melbourne from the country was not immediately at home in the prosperous, developing city; he was lonely. True, the law was a study that fascinated him and occupied the deductive side of his mind, but man does not live by law alone, not an O'Dowd at any rate. He needed food for his emotions, something, as he said, that could hold his confidence. Even knowledge for its own sake was not wholly self-sufficient. A. G. Stephens, in his introduction to the anthology *A Southern Garland,* indicated some of the milestones along the road to confidence:

To his active, ascetic mind no knowledge came amiss. He is at once learner and teacher, studying law, history and religion, interested in spiritualism, socialism, communism, anarchism, and mysticism, and holding fervent Sunday classes on all manner of subjects from poetry to ethics.

Until Fred Woods took him to the Melbourne Lyceum "Hall of Science" one Sunday afternoon, O'Dowd spent much of his spare time in long walks to the beach at Brighton to the place where Adam Lindsay Gordon had shot himself:

> Upon the beach at Brighton
> I listened to the sea,
> I thought of poor dead Gordon,
> The thought was sad to me.
>   Far, far from home of childhood,
>   In this weird lonely clime,
>   With self-inflicted vengeance,
>   He died before his prime.

The Lyceum membership was made up mainly of spiritualists and secularists with a sprinkling of anarchists for flavor. As can be imagined, they disagreed on many fundamental issues, but were united in the face of a general hostility towards the odd, the eccentric, and the unusual. Their textbook was the *Lyceum Leader* which contained a catechism—"What is the Lyceum? The school of a liberal and harmonious education. What is its object? The unfoldment of all the faculties in their due order and degree." To a person given to delirious enthusiasms and strange interests, the Melbourne Lyceum was just the place in which to indulge them. Bernard O'Dowd was the man for the place with his "formidable reserves of scholarship, his disturbing fluency in argument," to support his materialist viewpoint.

At first he confined himself to debating such subjects as monarchy versus republicanism, or lecturing on "Practical Christianity" and "The Early Days of Victoria," in which his "masterly style showed that he was well acquainted with his subject." Before long he was regarded as the leader of those younger members who believed successful living was to be achieved without recognition of any supernatural world or forces.

"The Lyceum set out to attract the young, and organized activities that were not very relevant to the 'spiritual' part of its programme. In spirit these had something in common with the various Youth Movements of today. There were calisthenics, spectacular marching and dancing, a kind of outdoors ritual; there were also debates and group discussions, singing and general entertainments."[3] Calisthenics was "conducted with spirit and energy" by Miss Evangeline Fryer, a slight, dark, attractive girl nearly a year older than Bernard, who was both Vice-Conductor of the Lyceum and Leader of Debating. The Conductor was John Fryer, Eva's father, and the Treasurer, another of his daughters. O'Dowd lived at the Fryer home in Lygon Street, Carlton, and courted the lively, self-confident Evangeline.

Signs of a doctrinal split came in 1888 when Bernard was criticized for propounding snide atheism by refusing to admit that there was an intelligent and beneficient God, and the Fryers aroused suspicion not only because of the number of positions they controlled, but because they appeared more interested in the secular than the spiritual aspects of the Lyceum. Prior to the formation of a breakaway movement, however, O'Dowd was appointed editor of a new manual to be called *The Australian Secular Lyceum Tutor,* an anthology of verse and prose, maxim and precept. A part of the book was given over to methods of secular instruction and the remainder drew freely on sources as diverse as Shelley, Whittier, and nonconformist hymn-books. Over twenty unsigned poems by the editor were included in this production.

O'Dowd's intention was to make a book whose influence would be "morally elevating and mentally suggestive": "From the gardens of all the ages the choicest flowers have been culled, the purest sentiments gathered, so that the book will be interesting at home, as well as instructive in Lyceum sessions. I have had to use the pruning-knife frequently, for as the fairest trees often nourish fungi, so the most beautiful thoughts are at times tainted with the microbes of superstition."

IV. *Love, Light, and Liberty*

His biographers do not find any of the *Tutor* poems worth discussing individually and confine themselves to generalities: "They are hortatory and rhetorical: they use earnest, threadbare phrases in a time-honoured way: in the fulfilment of his task the schoolteacher dominated the poet. And in the attempt to be morally elevating little attention was paid to what might prove mentally suggestive."[4] It was left to E. Morris Miller, in a study of the poet's early writings, to suggest the value of the contributions to the *Tutor:*

His grasp of the philosophical naturalism and materialism of the
nineteenth century was no mean achievement for a young man who
was then only at the beginning of his university career. We have
here the sources of the ideas, which O'Dowd argumentatively and
skilfully patterned into the quatrains of *Dawnward?*[5]

In the *Tutor*, O'Dowd writes "Hoist the Flag":

> Hoist the flag, the good old flag!
>   Let this your motto be,
> Shining on your banner bright,
>   "Love, Light and Liberty."[6]

This motto, Miller explains, refers to love of home and family,
light that is found in knowledge, and liberty that makes for
happiness. "Bacchus" claims we

> Shall raze the walls of Babylon,
>   And build, yea, in a night,
> Man's new Jerusalem upon
>   Love, Light and Liberty![7]

The sestet of "A New Tertullian" (Collected *Poems*, p.166),
shows how the same basic motto has been transmuted from a
simple need for human freedom from bigotry, oppression, and
mental slavery:

> No! listen to the Poet Blue above
>   Carolling "God is Good! is ever nigh!
> There is no sin, no darkness! all is well!
>   He is in you, in me, is Life, is Love!"
> Carolling "God is Liberty!" And I
>   Believe because it is impossible!

Again, in a poem of 1910, O'Dowd used the very same motto in
yet another setting:

> The Kingdom of our Lady's noon is free
> To you who will her morning burden bear;
>   And to her love, her light, her liberty,
> She calls the fit of all the world to share.[8]

CHAPTER TWO

Words From the Master

THERE were two major influences on Bernard O'Dowd as a writer. Sydney Jephcott's literary and personal friendship helped him "realise what poetry really was both formally and substantially," but foremost in position and importance was Walt Whitman. A few months prior to O'Dowd's death in 1953 he wrote a brief tribute to those, "apart from omnivorous reading and a very loyal cohort of mates," to whom he felt indebted. "The wonderful stimulus of my communion with Walt Whitman," he said in the Preliminary Note to Hugh Anderson's bibliography of his work, "redeemed me from a growing disgust with the tinkling cymbalism of so much of what was then 'modern' verse and implanted in me a sense of both the real meaning of democracy and of the revolutionary functions and power of true poetry."[1]

It was Thomas Bury, a journalist working for the Ballarat *Courier*, who introduced young O'Dowd to the American's *Drum Taps* in 1885, at a time when he was seemingly uncertain of his purpose in life; "at a time," his biographers claim, "when he was trying to reconcile his notions of great poetry with the life about him and the warm humanistic impulses he wanted to express."[2] Whatever may have been Bury's reason for bringing Whitman to the Australian's notice, the meeting was fruitful, for Whitman soon grew to dominate the emotional side of O'Dowd's mind and a well-thumbed copy of the Canterbury Poets was always in his coat pocket. So much so, among his friends it became the standard greeting to ask if he had his "dirty little Walt" with him.[3] Some years later, O'Dowd took to wearing a piece of grass in his buttonhole as a symbol of loyalty to the *Leaves of Grass* men and one of his literary friends caught the gesture in a four-lined verse:

> A weed beside the gutter's edge
> That no one else would stoop to cull
> He took, and wore it as a pledge
> That Nature's works were wonderful.

I. *The Epic of Man*

On Saturday afternoons O'Dowd's habit was to take long walks and read Whitman's poetry. His diary for 1888 always notes when he had been "reading Walt."[4] A picnic with the Fryer family was never complete unless accompanied by verse from Whitman. He was their favorite poet. Then, as the more advanced literary persons began to notice the American and talk about his work at small gatherings, it became necessary to defend their "prophet and apostle."

On August 22, 1888, O'Dowd and Fred Woods attended a lecture at the Australian Church Debating Society meeting. Francis Adams, a radical English visitor to Australia, made slighting references to Whitman, and in retaliation Bernard drew a comparison between the poet of democracy and Shakespeare as "the bard of feudalism." In this, as in many other instances, he was simply following the American, who spent much time in accusing Shakespeare of not being a democrat, not one of "us."

At the Boxing Day picnic at Sandringham that year, O'Dowd felt happy and contented for the first time for many years. The family parties gathered under the ti-trees, the naked little boys bathing at the water's edge, were seen to be people: he felt their presence and their activities "as a broadened poem—an open ode to humanity." Walt Whitman, more than any other person, had warmed the bookish imagination; the fully liberated feelings of the law clerk would flow outwards over the whole Australian continent and arouse a sense of his own possible role as a patriot-prophet who would celebrate her virtues and mend her faults. "Whitman came as a clean hot wind, blowing the cobwebs and dust of ages before it and drying the mists that had been settling over the low-lying flats of contemporary literature."[5]

Early in 1889, while picking over the book-counters of some city shop, O'Dowd discovered a selection of the beloved Walt's poetry, sympathetically introduced by William Rossetti. The diary entry for that day notes that the purchased book was first published in 1868. It was probably no coincidence that under the same date O'Dowd indicates he was "thinking of a great epic on Man, showing his birth from the lower powers of nature, his vicissitudes and triumphs." The thought has the appearance of being stimulated by Whitman, and may be considered the seed that bloomed nearly twenty years afterwards in a theory of poetry whose function was "to fill the people with a sense of their creativeness and to grapple, in its own way, with all tendencies inimical to their well-being."[6]

II. *Whitman for the Soul*

Besides walking with Walt at the week-end Bernard thought to share his bliss with his friends. Already, at what was known as the "ethical class," a group led by O'Dowd was discussing Herbert Spencer's *Data of Sociology* section by section. Spencer was a discovery second only to Whitman, and the diarist is enthusiastic about these twin carburettors of the mind as "Spencer for the intellect and Whitman for the soul!" If Spencer deserved a discussion group, Whitman was worthy of an important position in a "literary symposium." This idea followed the purchase in March of *November Boughs*, but it was not until the middle of May, 1889, that the necessary arrangements for the meetings were made.

The inaugural meeting of the "Australeum," a combination of Austral and Lyceum, took place at Ernest Buley's home in the outer suburb of Canterbury. Eight members joined tongues over Arnold's *Light of Asia*. The following week, their number increased by one, discussion centered on *Wilhelm Meister*. By the July meeting the membership had grown to a total of twelve earnest students. One is not surprised to read in the diary of 1889 that O'Dowd confessed ardent wishes to be a poet or politician, perhaps both.

The desires were quite natural: Spencer's work indicated a possible reconciliation of Science and Religion, a social amity; Whitman spoke a new language and brought attention to the possibility of a national idiom. "The content of Whitman's poetry combined with the unconventional prose rhythms to carry him off his feet; they called to his poetic pulse which had already been tuned up and prepared for their acceptance by long reading of the Bible—the Hebrew psalms, the Song of Solomon, Ecclesiastes—and the Apocrypha."[7]

In mid-July the literary group was introduced to the Preface to *Leaves of Grass*, but O'Dowd fancied that his fellow members did not understand what it was about. Nevertheless, the poetry of Walt was accounted a "grand success." For twelve shillings he obtained a complete edition of *Leaves of Grass* with the "Children of Adam" added—the Songs of Sex as O'Dowd usually called them. To his diary he confided his opinion of their startling quality—"cannot say I have grasped them yet,

don't think they can be read by everyone." A present-day reader
is more likely to be amused by these poems which once aroused
violent passions. Their main appeal to O'Dowd is likely to have
been their combining of the attitudes of the proletarian radical
with those of the urban intellectual.

III.   Revered Master

Early in August he took a long walk beyond the suburb of
Kew to enjoy the fresh air and read Walt. The combination of
poetry and ozone caused him to record that he felt nobler and
that a "mighty tide of music-tinged thought-waves roll into my
soul." The young man's soul must have been attuned to the
music of the spheres, since he was almost tone-deaf to earthly
music, and was the only Australian poet, said E. J. Brady, who
sang "God Save the Queen" to the tune of "The Wearing of
the Green!" However, the high tide of thought-waves washed
up the meaning of Whitman's "songs of procreation"; we "must
go to them," O'Dowd thought, "as an anatomist to a naked
woman—[they are] not songs of lust but of the creation of
great individuals."

Three days after this particular Saturday stroll, O'Dowd
drafted the opening of a letter to his "Revered Master":

I have been going to write to you often but I feared being a pre-
sumptuous intruder. I am so now, I suppose, but after many unavail-
ing searches I have at last got a complete edition of your "Leaves of
Grass", & its might has impelled me to waft my sincerest thanks to
you—great Scald of Demos. I wish that I could put myself into this
sheet to shake hands with you, as you have put yourself into your
writings and blessed me. I shall not tire you with a description of
myself beyond saying that I am 23, impulsive but unenergetic, aspir-
ing but too often resting with aspiration, studious, solitary but loving
& working for the masses of men, fond of philosophy, poetry, science,
comparative history (in fact all comparative studies), with not enough
ambition to push myself on in the world, & passionately fond of Walt
Whitman (too much, I think, sometimes, for I find myself defending
your very faults) Solitary, I had said, yet with a young girl whom I
love and with three mates whom I reckon as a part of myself—otherwise solitary.

I used to write lines with the last words jingling similarly, in feeble
imitation of similar jinglers, but little since I have met with you,
Walt (I know you well, though you don't know me: we go out long
walks together on fine Saturday afternoons and you make the leaves

of grass and of the trees speak as none else can. For ages yet shall you so walk with young men out for their afternoon holiday.)

"Tom Touchstone" a Ballarat man, first introduced you to me. He is similar in some respects to yourself, with a touch of Thoreau about him. He loves you much, I think[8]

This letter was never completed, and so, never sent, but in March 1890, O'Dowd did pen an idolatrous missive to the pain-wracked, white-bearded, profit-poet in Camden, New Jersey:

Dear Walt, my beloved master, my friend, my bard, my prophet and apostle

I must write something to you now. I have tried during four years, but was not satisfied with my effort. Let my earnest will compensate for the clerk in a law library I know, & it would be presumption on my part to write to any stranger in this way, but you are not a stranger to me, you are my dearest companion: and, if you feel displeased, you have brought it on yourself for none who understandingly read you can help loving you. I am not going to praise your poetry to you (we don't usually tell the sun that he does well to shine & shines well, nor the grass do we praise for being green) & in regard to your other writings will only say that your hint re sun-baths has saved me many a day's illness & your essay on Carlyle has told me once a wanderer in the desert scorched by a material sun, that there is a night too glowing with star-life (in a word it caused me to study Hegel).

Sometimes I take myself out of myself & gaze at what is going on in my mind. I often notice that I am defending you even when this unbiassed apart-Ego know or believe that you are a little wrong. We have great fights over you sometimes. My mates & I myself try to spread you everywhere & we find that every reverent student gets to love you while those who merely glance at you are sometimes nearly as virulent against you as those of your maligners who have never read you at all. I think we have profited morally also from your indirections. You have driven away a good deal of pessimism from us & we can now work lightheartedly in our small spheres. I was a Roman Catholic once, & had been, thus, for generations under pessimistic influence that the revelations of science could not drive away. My personal mates are Fred Woods, a draper, Jim Hartigan a plasterer, an adorer of you, Ada Fryer a boot-shop assistant (my sister-in-law) Ted Machefer (a scapegrace, a swagman only, but a true mate of 11 years standing) & my wife. I am 24, red hair, plain features, a little too backward for my own good, fond of poetry, philosophy, science & going long walks, (I have got together a philosophy class of workmen & workwomen mainly & the avidity with

which the revelations are seized is a pure pleasure to witness. My
mates all send their love & I do so, enclasped by my own. . . .

I don't want to give you trouble, & so, as your correspondence
must be extensive, will not expect an answer, honoured as I would
feel by one. I sincerely hope that your physical life is happy now &
that pain does not alloy your spiritual glory.

With a "handful out of my heart"
Good by Walt,
So Long!
Bernard O'Dowd

P.S. "Tom Touchstone" (Mr. Bury) a journalist in Ballarat, & like
you in many respects, first introduced you to me.

Whitman, touched probably by the simple assurance that his
words had a liberating power in far-away Australia, replied almost immediately. His letter came to the Supreme Court Library
like "a burst of heaven." O'Dowd hastened to write the first of
his "good, long, varied and loving" letters to his "dear Master"
in which he inflicts the story of his twenty-four years and depicts
bush life in Australia. There is no deep intellectual exchange
in this correspondence between two men of such disparate back-
grounds and ages, but there is a depth of intimacy, a warm
communication of spirit between them. It was to remain an inspiration to O'Dowd throughout his life and rises like an emotional yeast in his poetry.

CHAPTER THREE

The Burning Bush

THE EARLIEST poem in *Dawnward?* in respect to first publication[1] is "Compromise." For a writer who "wasted no time over the niceties of verse"[2] there is a healthy muscular strength in this poem; a careful and precise use of general images. O'Dowd's object[3] has been to concentrate his effect in the fewest possible words with a sparing use of the definite article in favor of active verbs, nouns, and adjective phrases.

Inglis Moore considered "there is no picture in [the metaphors], nothing sensuous, no retinal impression. They remain ideas rather than true images."[4] Certainly, much poetry is visual or it is tedious, but it may be visual by virtue of its imagery or by virtue of its action. Rarely does O'Dowd keep his verses tied to the merely informative or conceptual level; the appropriateness of his technique is easily seen in his word structure:

> I pencil glaring wings of Right
> With Wrong's sedater black;
> And rushing Freedom's crotchets with
> Resurgent minims slack.

The writer does not depend too much on likeness in the things he compares. He is just to the complexity of his experience and there is a certain "tough-minded" integrity in the essential clash of his comparisons. This suits the ironic context of the poem. As a general principle, this can be illustrated by his use of metaphor and the care given to the selection of words in re-writing "Compromise" for publication in *Dawnward?*[5] "The cataract of vengence, due/For age old crimes of caste" became "The gales of vengence on the ripe/Enormities of caste." A line in the original manuscript[6] that read "And slacken froward Duty's pace/With rosy interest," was changed to "For froward Duty hesitates/When wrongs grow vested rights."

I. *Nuptials of Hell*

O'Dowd also changed a weak line in the manuscript version from: "I put a pretty hectic on/The pallor of the Wise," to "And put sophistic hectics on/The pallor of the Wise."

The use of "sophistic" in the fourth verse focusses the meaning clearly on the deceptive nature of compromise, the removal of the indefinite article helps make the image particular, and the personification acts as a guard against a tendency to over-simplification.

In a number of instances, O'Dowd was not successful in his attempts to change verses intended for book publication, but in the last stanza of "Compromise" he has tightened and strengthened the conclusion. The *Bulletin* version spoke of:

> Insipid grace of love I lead
> To lust's lip's hydromel;
> Or twine the snow-cold heaven with
> The glowing limbs of hell.

In revision, the awkward second line has been removed, and in keeping with the speech of Compromise, the non-intoxicating hydromel, which is the raw material of honey, has been attached to Love rather than Lust. The fifth and final verse now stands as:

> My brews that change to mead of Lust
> Love's vapid hydromel,
> Should tempt the very seraphim
> To nuptials of hell.

There is a faint "echo" here of Walter Landor's poem "Under the Lindens."

When writing "Compromise," Bernard O'Dowd had in his mind the admiration he felt for Justice Higginbotham, whom he regarded as one of the few men holding public office at the time who would never compromise. The earliest draft manuscript included another stanza that referred to so many conservative thinkers of the period:

> I soften Freedom's clarion
> With fluting Sentiment
> Persuade Reform the right road is
> Whereon old Error went.

Some readers may consider the lack of any organic development is an important weakness in "Compromise," but an argument could be made out that this is not a weakness but an essential condition for the kind of expression aimed at by the writer. In pursuing the truth of individual fact, the single and almost self-contained individualities that a poem discovers, O'Dowd was illuminating, not developing, ideas.

Undoubtedly, O'Dowd saw himself as the revealer of truth and the shepherd of the poor and the exploited: "The kestrel shepherd of all weaker birds,/Compact of thought and lithe with lightning words,/Their enemies to harry and pursue . . .".[7]

In the "Song of Hate" he expresses much the same thought:

> I scour the present and the past
>   In tyrant-hunting raids;
> No weakling in the flocks of caste
>   My vulture-sight evades.[8]

II. *Song of Hate*

"Hate," to an even greater degree than "Compromise," employs astonishing descriptive phrases, forceful verbs, and adjectives precisely employed for sharp strokes of meaning. Towards the end of the poem there is a change in the verse structure and a flexibility of rhythm in keeping with intense indignation: "Hatred regards not only particular individuals but universals; it is incurable and seeks to damage and not merely vex; anger may at length be satisfied, but hatred never."[9]

The poem as it now appears in the collected edition of *Poems* (pages 44-45) has, like "Compromise," been strengthened by the expansion of what was originally the fourth verse:

> When Liberty salaams to Fate,
>   And Havoc's typhoons blow,
> I kiss the shoulders of the great
>   And Envy's vipers grow.[10]

to read:

> When titled Fraud with cant deludes
>   The mob, his neck I strip,
> And point where treason's asp protrudes
>   From print of Eblis' lip.
> When Liberty salaams to Fate,
>   I fling her gorging foes
> Gold apples labelled "For the Great!"
>   Till Envy murder grows.

O'Dowd wrote an explanation of these lines to A. G. Stephens[11] in 1903: "'Envy's vipers grow'—The image is from the *Shah*

Nameh where Iblis kissed the tyrant Zobale's shoulders and 'from the touch spray two black serpents.' I think 'grow' is justified, although the meaning is not, perhaps, as obvious as it might be to the reader unacquainted with the legend."

In the same letter the poet refers to the line, "Although my sister, Love, is God," as the Bible story "imbedded in our literature," and comments that hate, though terrifying, may conceal or symbolize Love which is God's very self. "As God speaks from or from about the bush, so Love of Man may be the real meaning after all, of that Hate that decimates the enemies of man."

Passion lends flexibility to the rhythm, with the caesuras falling in various feet:

> When Freedom's legions, wearied, nod,
> Relentless on I push.
> Although my sister, Love, is God,
> I am the burning bush.

The image in the final verse of "Hate," derived from the parable of the tares, is one commonly met in O'Dowd's verse.[12] These lines have had attention from the "careless" poet; in the manuscript version the reading was merely "poetic":

"And I, who choke with seeding bane/The lushest dells of wrong,"

but all the printed copies have been made particular and forceful:

> And I, who choke with seeding bane
> The pastureage of Wrong,
> Demand a niche in Freedom's fane,
> A verse in Freedom's song.

III. *Nervous Mythology*

Many criticisms of the *Dawnward?* verses have been expressed by those who seek an enfeebled romantic life in poetry, rather than a vivid, close and searching impact. Some have missed the working distinction between "picture" and "image-proper"—the latter being commonly brought in by metaphor and comparison—because O'Dowd usually neglects the more conventional visual image in favor of the emotional power and directness of auditory, tactile, and muscular images. Generally, critics have overlooked the fine work in this first book,[13] although the *Bulletin* did say, "The first collection had the effect of a cannonade, and was witnessed with respect."[14] The same weekly had previously concluded a review of *Dawnward?* in expressive terms: "O'Dowd's bronze does not always run freely; but when it does he moulds a statue."[15]

Bernard O'Dowd, in private conversation, informed the writer that he was so strongly influenced by biblical and ancient history that he felt mythology to be part of his nerves; in some manner it was seized upon as material with which to incarnate his emotion and so create meaning. The poet sought to restore a forgotten unity: "These fables are like corpses which, fortunately for us, remain visible after their living content has departed out of them. In the *Classical Dictionary,* the student of poetic diction finds delicately mummified for his inspection any number of just those old single meanings."[16]

Perhaps O'Dowd's greatest single attribute as a poet is his ability to handle subsidiary meanings—and his mastery of metaphor. As needed, he passes from allegory to symbolism, from direct statement to prophetic foreboding innuendo; he can present a situation and, by his care with words, at the same time move a responsive reader by means of undercurrents of thought, association, and mood. Some of his most telling effects are achieved by concentrating attention on familiar things, making them stand out suddenly against an unfamiliar background. This he does by the use of strictly technical words and by sustained symbolism, quite often producing a sense of strangeness:

It [allegory] is the art of expressing a relation between things which is not ordinarily perceived; it is the art of throwing a strong light on aspects of the world which are ordinarily disregarded, or of placing what is familiar in an atmosphere which will reveal something unexpected and unknown in the most unlikely places; to it men have recourse when their thoughts seem to have outrun the ordinary and accepted modes of expression.[17]

The emotional pressure of his feeling and his social thinking caused O'Dowd to telescope the ancient past and political present. Nevertheless, he was very definite as to the immediate ends to be sought. Writing of the social climate in 1897, he pointed out "that until we have created our own social atmosphere we must continue to be oppressed by the mephitic vapours of the present plutocratically created social atmosphere. We must have our own ideals and work towards them, uninfluenced by the more garish show of 'orthodox' ideals; we must develop our criterions of honour, our own chivalry, our own social sur-

roundings, our own literature and art."[18] This view informs
almost all the "early" poems, and is, indeed, a keynote throughout O'Dowd's public life.

"The Seed Time" is a most unfortunate piece of poetic patch-
work, due directly to the advice of critic A. G. Stephens, who
suggested that the original poem was not in keeping with scientific theory.[19] In protest, O'Dowd pointed out he was

aware before writing it of conflicting theories (Spencer's Centralian
experience since is also against me) but as I was not pretending to
write an exact treatise (I) conceived I had the right to adopt Curr's
theory for my vatic purpose, especially as a Westralian eye-witness's
experience of a ceremony appeared to me good evidence of that
theory being a true one in parts at least of Australia. I would regret
elision of scenery as it entered somewhat into my "atmospheric"
scheme.[20]

IV. *The Scattered Seeds*

The poem centers upon a quotation from Psalms—"he would
overthrow their seed among the nations, and scatter them in the
lands"[21]—and on O'Dowd's reading of E. M. Curr's *Australian
Race*.[22] The latter discusses what has been termed "the Terrible
Rite" and was referred to when the poem first appeared:

In some parts the subjects of the rite are chosen by a cruel process
of scoring the back with pieces of flint; in others the whole tribe is
subjected to some form of the rite. Its origin is lost in mystery.
Danton's Punic or Adonic theory appears to be quite new. Whatever
may be its origin, it is the strangest ceremony of a strange race, which,
however degraded it may seem to some, reckons it better to die out
as a race altogether rather than accept our civilisation.[23]

Before book publication, what was originally a seventeen-
stanza poem entitled "The Land of the 'Terrible Rite'" was
severely revised and reduced to twelve stanzas, five of which
are entirely new. Neither version is altogether satisfactory, but
the *Tocsin* poem has structural lines, a grouping, development,
and progression of theme, lacking in *Poems*. As a whole, the
poem is marred by a slight woodenness and two forced and flat
concluding quatrains.

The nightmare scene in a harsh devouring land is set in the
two opening stanzas:

> 'Mid spiny grass and ashen leaves
> The ranges granite teeth protrude:
> A strange repulsive orchid weaves
> Its slimy plots for living food.
>
> Harmattans, bell-drawn, dim with dust
> The bronzy green of spectral trees;
> Sad salt lakes swoon to desert's lust,
> And poison flowers entice the bees.

The aboriginal inhabitants and the ordeal of the rite fit the primitive and oppressive land:

> Its scanty niches hold a race
> With brand of Desolation burned,
> On whom, mayhap, in primal days
> The "evil eye" of God was turned.
>
> Their paltry rights of love and food
> From surging Future's claim to shield,
> The gods unto them wise and good
> A fearful ordeal had revealed.
>
> They rob the Fate-accursed boy,
> Who flinches while its tortures vex,
> Of all but merest dregs of joy,
> Of Holy Plentitude of Sex.

The poem pauses while the author gathers his parallel commentaries; is this rite a punishment for past social crimes? First, there is the biblical example:

And they served their idols; which became a snare unto them: Yea, they sacrificed their sons and their daughters unto demons, And shed innocent blood, even the blood of their sons and of their daughters, whom they sacrificed unto the idols of Canaan. . . .[24]

O'Dowd has rejected the ceremonial ornamentation theory in favor of a "Punic" explanation drawn from history:

> Does a Carthage atone for the breach of trust
> In the plutocrat days of its might,
> With its women reserved as a latrine for lust,
> And its men for the 'Terrible Rite'?

In the eighth stanza he intersects his two comparisons in an image of Australia prostituted by capitalism. What happens to

an individual in a rite can be the fate of a whole population
in an evil social system:

> Far-fetched? Yet some such doom awaits
> E'en alien races in this land;
> In putrid grandeur at its gates,
> See, youthful harlot cities stand!

At this point, what might loosely be called the recitative closes
and the aria begins, and the contemporary parallel is developed.
The version in *Poems,* although adequate for the requirements
of the new closing lines, does not "key" into the printed poem
as it did in "The Land of the 'Terrible Rite.'" This may be seen
more clearly when the two are set down together:

> The ragged child, the foodless man
> In every city street abound.
> The air itself seems under ban,
> Some curse infects the very ground!
>   *Tocsin*

> The foodless child, the sterile dame
> In every city's streets appear,
> And workhouse roofs already shame
> The palaces of pride we rear.
>   *Poems*

"The ragged child, the foodless man" fits "miles of wool and
grain" much better than "the foodless child, the sterile dame";
also, the last two lines of the *Tocsin* poem recall the poisoned
Harmattan winds of the second verse and prepare for the introduction of mephitic gases two verses later.

Actually, O'Dowd's poem had a statistical basis drawn from
a medical report, printed in part in the *Tocsin:* "The marriage
rate is steadily decreasing; the age at which men marry is rising; the number of births per marriage is decreasing." Excluding
prostitutes, it was estimated that one in every twenty-three
women in Victoria was a "concubine."[25] A fortnight later, with
an apposite remark, the newspaper returned to the subject. "We
talk about the inhumanity of the savage. Let us have a look at
ourselves before we decide on our superiority. The benighted
heathen would, for his opportunities, put us to the blush (if
that were possible)."[26]

V.   *The Swag of Woe*

For no apparent reason the poet altered what originally read as a very appropriate image into a vague and inconsequential one: "Its bands of wifeless men migrate/With heavy swags of wearying woe/And souring billies full of hate," became: "Its bands of wifeless men migrate/With sagging loads of care and woe/And meagre wallets soured with hate,"[27] the first having a precision and continued reference in the verse that follows in both cases.

"The Land of the 'Terrible Rite'" grinds to a stop in an unfortunate descent in tone to the language of political cliché:

> While the millstones of Mammon continue to grind
> And injustice's locusts to blight,
> Can we feel that to savage is confined
> The disgrace of the "Terrible Rite"?
> Ev'ry person, succumbing in childless despair
> In our brutal competitive fight,
> Is a victim our hyprocrite apathies tear
> With the flints of a "Terrible Rite."

An attempt might be made to justify lines such as those above on the grounds that they have been prepared for throughout the poem. In replacing them, O'Dowd added five more verses making an extended use of the myth of Hercules fighting off the Stymphalian birds. So, he argues, shall democratic reform overcome social injustice. Good as they may be, the lines do not really belong in the poem, and for balance and honest expression, for sincerity, preference must be given the *Tocsin* poem; while it is not a completely successful, and certainly not a great poem, it is a significant one. The following year O'Dowd entered his talents directly on the side of political verse.

CHAPTER FOUR

Poet and Politician

ALTHOUGH Australia was still in the pre-industrial stage in the last decade of the nineteenth century, city manufacturing ventures were increasing in importance. The gold discoveries of the fifties had given local industry a head start by providing a sudden increase in consumers and had helped concentrate skilled labour in the towns; the population movement was from countryside into the towns, from agriculture to industry. One economic historian considered the employers at the time believed "the first step was to put down pretensions of wage workers to a share in the control of industry, the next was to consolidate a middle class of small producers."[1]

At the end of the century, the national scene was not inspiriting; the buoyant tide that had seemed to sweep in towards true democracy was already ebbing. The inspiration of Utopian dreams faltered in the face of economic realities such as steadily falling prices, paralysing drought, and lockouts and strikes.

The new industrial mode of production, tied though it was to primary manufacture, had even then given rise to numerous social abuses. To expose such abuses and to serve as a focus for the labor viewpoint, O'Dowd and two others agreed to found a radical weekly newspaper to be named the *Tocsin*. The newspaper, while it supported labor, was in no sense completely partisan and gave strong emphasis to matters such as education and general reforms beyond the range of immediate politics.

Each of the three had valuable contacts in union circles and artistic groups, and with the financial support of the Trades Hall, formed a co-operative to control the newspaper. Hugh Corbett, Jack Castieau, and Bernard O'Dowd were the editors, which meant, said O'Dowd, that they were not paid.

All three, however, were secure in positions within the Victorian public service; Castieau in the Chief Secretary's office, Corbett in the Mint, and O'Dowd at the Crown Law Department. The manager of the newspaper, George Prendergast, was a printer by trade and a democratic battler who had been the first secretary of the Labor Party in 1892 and was then a member of the Legislative Assembly representing North Melbourne. Prendergast was assisted on the technical and printing side by E. Findley, another rising parliamentarian in Victoria's State legislature.

The *Tocsin* platform totalled seventy-four items, some reflecting the influence of Henry George, Edward Bellamy and the British Fabian socialists, but most were formulated from local labor experience and gave expression to the demands of the trade union movement.[2] Their leading idea, however, was that industrial action alone was insufficient, and the workers needed, in addition, an independent political party to lead them in their struggle. Not that there was anything very revolutionary about the *Tocsin* platform. One gentleman was reported to have said they could all be realized without upsetting the stability of the country, except number sixty-three, "The Purification of Sport."[3]

The first issue appeared October 2, 1897, with a poem by Victor Daley on the front page in which he invoked the bells of St. Antoine that heralded the French Revolution.

I. *The Warning Voice*

Apart from verse and more general articles, O'Dowd contributed a regular column, "The Forge," under the name of "Gavah the Blacksmith." The headpiece to the feature was drawn by the artist, Lionel Lindsay, from a living model in a nearby blacksmith's shop and was followed by a quotation from Firdusi's epic Persian poem, "Shah Nameh":

> Gavah, meanwhile, with warning voice set forth
> What wrongs the nation suffered, and there came
> Multitudes round him, who called out loud
> For "Justice! Justice!" On his javelin's point
> He fixed his leathern apron for a banner,
> And, lifting it on high, he went abroad
> To call the people to a task of vengeance.

"The Forge" was the means of giving advice on the political and industrial activities of the period, with O'Dowd drawing as needed on his legal training and wide reading for examples and support. It gave an opportunity to range over a wide field attacking complacency as well as injustice. Reading the hundreds of articles today, one gets the impression that O'Dowd was not then so much against the capitalist State as "unjust laws" and "biased" politicians, his politics at the time fluctuating be-

tween Reformism and Syndicalism. He looked to socialism as
an emotional unifying doctrine in the same manner as William
Lane:

Understanding Socialism will not make people at once what men and
women should be, but it will fill them with hatred for the unfitting
surroundings that damn us all, and with passionate love for the ideals
that are lifting us upwards, and with an earnest endeavor to be,
themselves, somewhat as they feel humanity is striving to be.[4]

Prior to the clashes with employers that took place in 1890,
unions had supplemented industrial action by lobbying and
petitioning members of Parliament in a sectional manner. The
election of men directly representing their interests subsequent
to the defeat of the strikes, meant simply the extension to State
Parliaments of the common striving to secure from government
measures for the alleviation of the workers' characteristic dis-
tress, but without abolishing that position. The Socialists took
the view that the Labor Party would spontaneously gravitate
towards socialism, and that ultimately Labor would win a majority in Parliament and would use this power to usher in the
the socialist era peacefully and without revolution. The day of
the *Tocsin's* coming marked the end of parliamentary groupings
created by conflicting personalities rather than divergent party
politics.

II.   *Federation*

There was also an impulse towards the federation of Australia's six States. Australians, the popular argument went, are one
people and it is necessary to have a federal government responsible for the country as a whole. Many genuine democrats,
among them the *Tocsin* editors, were deeply distrustful of the
proposals from the beginning and, after the early conferences
on the federal constitution, used their radical newspaper to
openly fight the issue with an outpouring of verse and prose
ranging from cool legal analysis to passionate declaration. Their
main opposition lay in the argument that the Federal Bill would
make any real improvement in the social system impossible for
generations to come.

While O'Dowd wrote articles on subjects as diverse as gam-
bling and pure foods, Sunday and social organization, it was
the current proposals for federation that occupied most of his

attention in the *Tocsin's* first year of publication. His first shot
in the campaign was fired late in 1897 when he pointed out
the insidious danger of the delegates being tempted to vote for
any kind of federal scheme for "the sake of the Fame which
will be accorded by the perhaps foolish Future to the 'successful' nation builders."[5] Two months later, he discussed the danger inherent in the clauses relating to trade between the States,
claiming that if five States had good factory laws and one bad,
the other five would be swamped by "tainted goods."[6] Both
articles were superficial in treatment and it was not until early
in the following year that he really showed what a detailed and
penetrating study he had made of the proposed Bill.

In renewing the campaign in 1898, the editorial column
sounded an ominous note: "There will be no escape from the
Federal Constitution, except by revolution; and that is the way
Australia is to be cornered. A patient people like the Australians
will suffer much before they take extreme measures, and it is
on this fact that the wanton constitution builders rely."[7] But
O'Dowd was not concerned with possibilities of revolution, only
with the immediate aim of parliamentary Labor. He began with
a question characteristic of his concern about ends and means
—"Is constitutional reform an end in itself, or is it the mere
means to an end?"—and decided that the answer given decides
"whether a man is a Liberal or a member of the Labor Party."
Constitutional reform, to this radical journalist, was a means of
fighting more effectively by replacing the "bows and arrows of
trades unionism" with cannon;[8] federation was to be bitterly
opposed because it did not modify the "evil constitutional system" of the States and because it was the intention of the
delegates to "dish" the State Labor Party completely.

Even so, quite apart from the politics of the moment, the
Tocsin was alarmed at opportunist tendencies amongst Labor
leaders, and called upon one of these to cease pursuing policies
"totally opposed to those of the Labor Party." When the campaign against federation was concluded, the subject was still
important to "Gavah": "Militant Labour must never forget that
it is militant, that it is engaged in a war to the death—Forget-
fullness of this has heretofore frequently brought about a re-
rivetting of Labour's chains by means of the place-hunter and
demagogue from its own ranks, and the sophist from the other
side."[9]

III. *Political Mud*

It is this view that informs verses in *Dawnward?* such as:

> Content with Freedom's forms, shall we
>   Real tyranny caress,
> Through sybaritic apathy
>   Or mad forgetfulness?

As S. E. Lee comments, "It was politics that made O'Dowd a serious poet for the second time."[10]

No rounded consideration of Bernard O'Dowd's poetry can afford to neglect the verse and prose dealing with the federal campaign, yet in itself, the verse is generally of low quality and rightly has not been reprinted. Little imaginative effort is required to understand it and it deals in the simplest and most easily aroused emotions. Apart from a few good images which glitter in a paste of political mud, almost all the verses are merely propaganda jingles, effective for the purpose, but of no lasting value and deserving of the stricture, "sub-standard verse rhetoric,"[11] levelled by James McAuley at the later work of O'Dowd.

A far greater achievement lies in the prose material, much of which analysed the proposed bill clause by clause. The analysis was almost entirely of legal and political factors, but places the issue of federation against the larger economic background in a manner unmatched by any other commentator of the time. More recently it has been pointed out that "by no means all of these factors were economic factors, but in one form or another most of them were associated with an economic motive."[12]

Of the dozen or so verse items contributed by O'Dowd "for crude, forceful propaganda"[13] purposes, not more than one or, possibly, two could stand apart from the political turmoil that gave them sustenance.[14] Their value here is that they illustrate the lingering political attitudes of the poet; long after the situation had changed, the images recur.

That the bill was the product of compromise was not excused by the leading delegate, Alfred Deakin; in fact, he said that "it is perhaps by a wise discretion that we have insufficiently and inadequately dealt with the difficulties. . . ."[15] Tom Tunnecliffe, a Labor Member of Parliament and writer for the *Tocsin*, however, detected in this statement "the iron hand beneath the glove of democratic formalism."[16] O'Dowd also used this cliché in a verse-parallel called "The Federal Plot":

> In new vice-regal velvet
> You've wrapped a Caesar's paw;
> You've perched upon their future
> The Vultures of the Law.[17]

In these four lines, O'Dowd points to the retention of power over Parliament by a Governor-General, and to the creation of a High Court "with power of interpretation equivalent to power of dictatorship," in that its judgement would be "referrable to no more definite standard than the personal opinion of the judge that declares it."[18]

The first of the recurring images is that of "chained labour":

> Victoria has her troubles,
>   Of minor bonds complains;
> I guarantee to cure her—
>   With stronger-welded chains,[19]

Two months later; he wrote, "Spurn their brand-new fetters/ Gilt with tommy rot," or, in the same verses, the line: "Legironed with despair."[20] Another month or so, and it appears again:

> Though from our ankles clinging yet
>   Are fetters of a wage,
> We're ravelled iron Thraldom's net
>   And opened Serfdom's cage.[21]

Almost two years later the same idea is used in "Proletaria":

> And here hangs Rent, that squalid cage
>   Within which Mammon thrusts,
> Bound with the fetter of a wage,
>   The helots of his lusts.[22]

Regarding the opportunist tendencies within the federal movement and those who left the cause "for a handful of silver," O'Dowd wrote in 1898:

> We've lost so much by lure and dole:
>   The pick of their brigades
> Were Sons of Labour, sucked of soul
>   By wet-lipped Mammon maids.
>
> Those Labour foreheads branded by
>   The Antichrists of Greed

> Were captains of a company
> Who left us in our need.
>
> ("Foreboding")

It was of this poem that O'Dowd wrote to A. G. Stephens in protest against its exclusion from *Dawnward?*:

I deeply regret that policy forbids this at least from finding a place. I have seldom felt inspiration as I did when I wrote that (I could hardly have written it re amended Bill. I opposed the 1st because I thought it meant plutocratic compounds out here: the 2nd mainly because I thought the States not quite ripe. Even yet, although I accept the present Commonwealth and am delightfully disappointed in its many falsifications of my fears up to date, I do not regret writing that piece and am afraid that the Ides of March have not quite gone. *Obsit omen!*) But we can't argue matters of policy.[23]

IV. *Seducing the Veterans*

"Proletaria," again, sounds the recurring note:

> The wet-lipped Lamias of Caste,
>   Awaiting our advance,
> Our choicest squadrons' fealty blast
>   With magic smile and glance:
>
> Delilah-limbed temptations flit
>   Among our drowsy rows,
> And on our willing captains fit
>   The badges of our foes.

In "Dawnward?" O'Dowd makes much the same point in this stanza:

> And "Comfort!" Will her siren song
>   To narcotizing shades
> Seduce our veterans, while Wrong
>   Our weaker frontiers raids?

Besides the repetition of images over several years' verse-writing there is a choice of language in keeping with his view of militant labor "engaged in a war to the death" against capitalism. An example from 1898 speaks "Of slowly-forward-pushing forts/Of palisades from Mammon won,/And sanguine skirmishers' reports."

A vestige of this remains in verses from "Dawnward?"

> Wherever Plenty's crop invites
> Our pitiful brigades,
> Lurk Cannoneers of Vested Rights,
> Juristic ambuscades.

Of the mass of verse O'Dowd contributed to the campaign against the referendum on federation, there are perhaps three with some value beyond the immediate political question. One, "Foreboding," has been quoted in part above. The second, "The stealthy squadrons of the foe," did not appear until the middle of 1899, when it was introduced by several inches of explanation of the role of the "Wooden Horse and the Sinons of Federation":[24]

> The stealthy squadrons of the foe
> Are ambushed round the wall,
> The vulture signals to the crow
> That Troy's about to fall.

In spite of the broadsheets, the street meetings, the articles and the verses, the Constitution Bill was affirmed by Australian voters. Federation became an actuality, and only in the amendment clause could the *Tocsin* see even remote possibilities "of the dawn of a free constitution in the distant future."[25] The bright vision of the future Australia that was to be delivered by political agitation was clouded by doubt. Sadly the *Tocsin* buried its hopes in the editorial column the following year:

The *Tocsin* bitterly opposed the passing of the Commonwealth Bill for what it deemed, and still deems, sound reasons. Its articles on the subject will be some evidence to an unbelieving future that there was some good in Sodom, and its elaborate criticism of each clause of the bill will live, along with Higgins's speeches on the subject. . . .

We were defeated, and now that the Bill has become an Imperial Act, we must accept the inevitable. . . .[26]

O'Dowd's third poem, while it too expresses the frustrations of defeat, indicates a belief in the ultimate triumph of labor aspirations:

> There's a rift within the lute, a cleavage in the rock,
> A canker in the rosebud of our power,
> An uncanny murmur soughs, a mysterious warning knock
> Disturbs our smug and placid midnight hour.

And the murmur rises, rises, hear it on the veldt,
   'Tis soughing through the banyan and the palm,
By the east and western shamrock is its breathing felt—
   To dead and dying nations it is balm.

For it whispers of our ruin, turns the hourglass down,
   And points how fast the shuddering seconds run,
And the dead and dying nations dream of new renown,
   When our eclipsing horror leaves the sun.[27]

CHAPTER FIVE

Democracy and Conscience

WRITING of "The Uncollected Poems of Bernard O'Dowd" in the special O'Dowd number of *Southerly*, S. E. Lee claimed that the poet's "complete preoccupation with militant labour politics, more than any other single circumstance, explains the tone of the *Dawnward?* . . . verses."[1] While the statement does carry considerable weight, equating these particular verses with a "need for crude, forceful propaganda" is an oversimplification.

In announcing the result of its sonnet competition, the *Bulletin* spoke of the winner as an "intellectual diamond, with a facet flashing in every line."[2] The sonnet, "Australia," the newspaper continued, "urges the question and doubt which state Australia's present place in the philosophic vistas"; it does, in effect, express how it feels to hold certain political opinions and it is also impossible to doubt that directly behind the poem lie the then advanced views of the *Tocsin* group. But this is not the same as saying the sonnet is overtly didactic.

"The sonnet," in Victor Kennedy's view, "has since become a classic, an ornament for anthologies and school text-books, but much casual handling has not taken the edge off its intensity. In concise words and images it formulated the question O'Dowd had often brooded over as he let his imagination range over the distant past of the ancient continent and then looked around him at the confused present, with its trivial conflicts and divided purposes."[3] This comment, while basically a true one, does not tell much either about the formulation of the question, as the writer expresses it, or about its success as a poetic statement.

As a contrast, and perhaps political balance, to "Australia" consider the sestet of another sonnet printed after the competition:[4]

> I call her 'maid'? Her fancy roams at large
> And pants for fornication where it lights,
>   Is it worth while, O God! to save or damn

The giddy nurse-girl turning from her charge
To talk with khaki-coated blatherskites
While "Federation" gurgles in the pram?

Here we have the bare bones of didacticism, with Australia as
the "giddy nurse-girl" flirting with a Boer War veteran while
the bastard child plays in its carriage.

I. *The Drifting Island*

The form of "Australia" is the rare, but acceptable, compromise between the Italian and the English sonnet; its pattern
may be stated as 4 : 4 : 3 : 3—a useful basis in this particular
example, since such a form allows variation of thought and
emotion yet retains the divisions and discipline of rhyme.
The first quatrain sets the central figure:

Last sea-thing dredged by sailor Time from Space,
Are you a drift Sargasso, where the West
In halcyon calm rebuilds her fatal nest?
Or Delos of a coming Sun-God's race?

Australia is the oldest continent, we are told by geologists, and
certainly the "last," or most recently discovered by the great
navigators. The word "dredged" has implications, not only of
the recovery of earth from the sea, but also refers generally
to the search for "sea-things," such as the dredging of plankton,
the first life-form, on the voyage of the *Challenger*. There is
also an implicit reference to "sea-thing" in *The Tempest* (Act
II, Scene 2). Again, this tremendous opening line introduces
ideas from philosophy with the poet equating space with surface and time as a line, and in combination with "sailor" conjures
up discoverers making time a movement in space. These details
sufficiently indicate the functional character of O'Dowd's imagery and the decisive language, potent with subsidiary meaning,
of the opening quatrain; the meaningful echoes have not entirely died in the mind when the closing line returns the reader
to the surrounding ocean. The method of recall also maintains
the closed form and configuration of the sonnet.

The remainder of this slightly contemptuous quatrain is packed
with precise reference in a rather complicated interweaving of
images drawn from mythology. "A drift Sargasso" forms a con-
nection with "sea-thing" of the first line and is, in turn, associated
not only with the idea of a floating island of sea-weed, but

with the lost continent of Atlantis. "Delos" in the ancient world was the floating island, which later became solid, where Apollo was born. Apollo, the sun-god, represents all the worthwhile arts and culture and O'Dowd's hopes for his settlement on the sun-drenched continent of Australia. Further, the mythical King-fisher, or halcyon, was said to nest in the Southern Ocean once a year, during which period the sea remained perfectly calm.

To a prejudiced reader all this detail might seem obvious or poetically unimportant, but lacking this referential background, the same reader misses a richness of texture, the movement and orchestration of the thought-laden emotion. "The poet's actual words give distinction and vitality to the thought, and therefore they are of the greatest importance, but there should be no emphasis on the words . . . at the expense of the thought, and above all no divorce of words and thought."[5] The argument of these four lines, that have taken almost fifty to explain, may be adequately expressed as a double-barrelled question: Is Australia a purposeless world where the exploitation and miseries of Europe are to be repeated, or re-built, or is she an augury of a new democracy?

> Are you for Light, and trimmed, with oil in place,
> Or but a Will o' Wisp on marshy quest?
> A new demesne for Mammon to infest?
> Or lurks millennial Eden 'neath your face?

II. *Omens and Auguries*

Dignified, but of lower intensity, the second quatrain is sub-ordinated to the first, and the eight lines are seen as two phases of the same experience. In rather trite and falsely "poetic" language O'Dowd sets out the questions; are we for knowledge and social progress, like the five wise virgins,[6] or is modern society wandering and vicious like the Will o' Wisp that lures men into the swamp of social injustice?

The sestet of the sonnet is carefully articulated to rise again in intensity to a climax and a rounded finish:

> The cenotaphs of species dead elsewhere
> That in your limits leap and swim and fly,
> Or trail uncanny harpstrings from your trees,
> Mix omens with the auguries that dare
> To plant the Cross upon your forehead sky,
> A virgin helpmate Ocean at your knees.

Again, there is considerable thought behind the surface images. A cenotaph is usually an empty tomb, but according to the poet, Australia is a living tomb, an omen of a dead world, with kangaroos, ganoid fish, and unique species of birds. Such are the omens. An augury is also a natural phenomena; in this instance, the harp-like musical sound O'Dowd claimed to have heard in the movement of the sheoak in the wind, but including also peripheral reference to: "We hanged our harps upon the willows in the midst thereof."[7]

The foremost sign of the new world, the Southern Cross, is not seen elsewhere and may be accepted as an augury. O'Dowd has brilliantly set off his reference to good and bad signs by allusions that spread and circle like ripples on a pond. "To plant the Cross upon your forehead sky"; the cross branded on Cain's forehead, or the cross of Christ's crucifixion? One recalls too, Stellamaris, the star of the sea, a title used in liturgies of the Virgin Mary, and a very apposite reference here. "Forehead sky" contrasts with the untouched ocean about the "knees," or shores of the continent, a "helpmate" ocean because Australia depended upon the sea for defence and communication. By this phrase the poet returns the reader to the "sea-thing" of the first line and completes the balance, at the same time changing the tone from slight distaste to one of exaltation.

III. *Democracy of the Mouth*

In the text of his much neglected lecture, "Democracy and Conscience," O'Dowd concluded that "Australian democracy is of the mouth only." [8] Nevertheless, he retained his confidence in a "general diffusion of true education" finally producing a "really noble democracy" in Victoria:

But, I must say that, from my study and experience of the last five or six years of Victorian affairs, political as well as intellectual and moral, I have got to be a little more pessimistic over the future than, as a democrat, I care to be. . . . I cannot shut my eyes to the increasingly numerous bad signs. The result is that at present I am in a state of doubt, but with a lean to the hopeful side, as to what is to be the outcome of things.

The reform movement was thought to be almost at the point of transition from the "dismal" darkness of apathy and ignorance into the "shining" light of faith and understanding; the direction, however, was not certain.

Some of the reasons underlying O'Dowd's "state of doubt" have been made clear in a sketch of the period written by his biographers:

It was a jingoistic and irresponsible period, with Teddy Roosevelt, the Rough Rider, talking of the power of the big stick in America; Cecil Rhodes, the manipulator of mining companies, being acclaimed a man of vision in England, and people everywhere surrendering to the mesmeric power of parades and circuses. O'Dowd had been affected by the easy way a majority of his countrymen had accepted a Constitution that might prove cramping yet indissoluble: he was more affected by popular support for the Boer War, a war that seemed to him a shameful adventure, prompted by greed for wealth and territory, yet using the most sacred symbols of patriotism and religion.[9]

Ignoring the lecturer's positive "lean," these commentators place his "emphasis on the side of doubt."

By "democracy" O'Dowd understood something more than political democracy; it was "that great modern tendency which is gradually and surely transferring political power, art, literature, knowledge, amusement, and all the things that go to make up life in the larger sense, from the possession of the privileged classes to that of the mass of the people." But without the guiding rein of a national conscience, which is "the average conscience of the individuals of the community," the rule of the majority over the minority is likely to produce "greater intellectual, moral, and spiritual degradation than the most odious tyranny. . . ."

> "Majority!" Divorced from wise,
> Sad conscience, will he prowl
> Through tender, human heresies
> With Torquemadan scowl?
> ("Dawnward?")

"The mob," O'Dowd believed, "is the danger-spot in Democracy's lungs." In the frenzied, sub-human mob the individual escaped from his responsible self, and it was the function of the poet "to turn the mob into a people, to exorcise the mob-spirit out of the people." O'Dowd "looked forward to the creation of a democracy so sensitive to moral issues that it would never think of using its power tyrannically." And the only way of creating such a democracy, he felt, was by "stimulating the conscience of its individual units."[10]

IV. *Campfires of the Lost*

While he passionately attacks the evils of society as he sees
them, the poet feels a strong sympathy for the unfortunate vic-
tims of ruthless industrialism. "The Campfires of the Lost"
throws a flickering light on the faces of the expendable:

> See there! a squeezed-out sponge of trade
> Or drunkard's, gambler's wife:
> And there! a haggard sempstress spayed
> By Competition's knife.[11]

This poem, seemingly apart from the terse stanzas of *Dawnward?*, is a chant in a single key so charged with emotion that
the ideas are submerged in the rhythm. The outcasts, feeding
their poor fires with "twigs and cones from dying Hopes," blas-
phemously and bitterly celebrate their black mass; "A diabolic
eucharist / With chalices of hate." Implacable verses of denun-
ciation end without a note of redemption:

> Ah, city dwellers! fearful wrong
> Entails a fearful cost,
> And ye that dare may see who throng
> Those bale-fires of the Lost.

His anger at the sight of "Proletaria" as "despised, polluted,
maimed and banned" fires his words with poetic flame:

> Ah, motherhood of misery
> For Christ-child as for pest!
> The greater her fertility
> The drier grows her breast! [12]

But he sees more than something requiring pity, for

> Tho' blind and dull 'tis we supply
> The painter's dazzling dreams;
> The rolling flood of Poetry
> From our dumb chaos streams.

O'Dowd's vision looked dawnward, and although he perceived
a society split into two camps, he believed there was hope of
the outcast mass producing poets, painters, and philosophers,
who would take up the cause of true democracy. "His clarion

call," Inglis Moore noted, "is to young democracy, but it is Australian democracy, and his burning democratic convictions are
mingled with the flames, up-shooting, of his hopes for his
country." [13]

V. *Man is God's*

In "Democracy and Conscience" O'Dowd maintained that the
true democrat saw in the least, the humblest, and the most sin-
ful, the capability of evolving the highest ideals. The least man
is a spiritual being and to the democrat, a sacred being, "a
wrong to whom is a wrong to the divine, a wrong to all."
"Young Democracy" remembers that Aesop, Epictetus, and Spar-
tacus were slaves:

> The prognathous Neanderthal,
>   To them, conceals the Bruce;
> They see Dan Aesop in the thrall;
>   From swagmen Christ deduce.

"The hedgeborn waif reminds [the democrat] of the manger-
born Christ, the street-girl calls up the sweet image of the Mag-
dalene. The horse-boy in yonder hotel-yard, cuffed and sworn at
by all and sundry, is not for him to cuff and swear at. For was
not glorious Shakespeare, too, a mere holder of horses in his
time?"

> They Jesus find in manger waif;
>   In horse-boys Shakespearehood:
> And earthquake-Luthers nestling safe
>   In German miner's brood.

To the true democrat men are essentially equal; "knowing that
when you balance the littleness of great men with their greatness, and the nobility of simple men with their littleness, God's
balances can scarcely prefer the one to the other." The mission
of those vowed to awaken their fellows to a sense of man's greatness must therefore not only teach but live the Golden rule of
Young Democracy:

> That each shall share what all men sow:
>   That colour, caste's a lie:
> That man is God's, however low—
>   Is man, however high.[14]

"This verse, given an emphasis by italics, may be taken as the centre of *Dawnward?* It combined terseness with lucidity, and in its positive note balanced the many question-marks of the book." [15]

CHAPTER SIX

Questions Without Answers

STRIVING to express his feeling about the future of Australia, on the dangers he saw about it, and the doubt whether it had justification for its democratic faith, O'Dowd made a rough draft:

Dawnward!

Out of the sluggish night where we too long
Have unrebellious waded through the mire
And 'neath the reckless stampedes of the strong
Seen all we loved expire!

Out of the dismal night where Faith and Hope
Were cunning lures to lead us astray
And niggard Duty limited in scope
And barred us from the Day!

Out of the eerie Night whose shivering gleams
Changed shadowy Doubt to huge and palsied Dread
Whose bodiless moans invaded all in dreams
Demon and vampire bred! [1]

The possible and subsequent shifts in the poem were merely jotted down in this order: Out of the brothel night; out of the diabolical night; out of the night where God is not; on to the pulsing dawn; on to the glow of dawn; on to the rose of dawn; on to where the sun, the sun is shining.

At the conclusion of "Democracy and Conscience," O'Dowd used the poem as printed in the *Bulletin*,[2] to illustrate his attitude and doubts:

I represent the people struggling in the gloom of night, through a sandy waste towards what they think is the dawn. The form of the clouds and other phenomena of night and gloom supply a sort of prophetic, enigmatical pantomime on their march, which, as my lecture has indicated, will be either towards brightness or towards deeper darkness, according as to the individual merits of the Democracy will it to be so or not.[3]

I. *Night into Day*

Using his central idea, the change from darkness to light, from night to day, the poet developed his thought by expansion and accretion from a vague and emotional wordiness to produce a poem that summarizes not only his own personal uncertainties but also something of the scepticism of the day. It appears from notes and the dates inscribed on a galley proof that A. G. Stephens, then literary editor of the *Bulletin*, received the proof early in December 1901, but being dissatisfied with several verses sent the copy to the poet for revision in the New Year. O'Dowd was on his annual holiday and did not receive Stephens' letter until the thirteenth of January, but replied the following day:

How would this do for first verse?
> That reddish veil which o'er the face
> Of Night-hag East is drawn—
> Flames new Disaster for (our, the) race,
> Or (may, can) it be the dawn?

4th verse
> Our flags with fetish watchwords glow.

5th verse
> Three watchwords! or as in copy

9th verse
> I don't think the "quotes" improve "equalities."

19th verse
Will Gog, awake, I prefer the comma also after Gog. Otherwise it is not clear whether "awake" is an adjective or a verb.

22nd verse
Lotus-heavy is not a word of mine. It seems foreign to my style somehow. If "lotus-eating," which expresses my meaning, is too vague or loose, I would prefer some such word as "narcotising." [4]

Stephens apparently queried the stanza:

> Will "Sport" educe a virile pith?
> Our pulses teach to throb?
> Or weary earth re-saddle with
> A Nika-riot mob?

One of O'Dowd's texts for an Arts degree subject was Gibbon's *Decline and Fall of the Roman Empire,* and sometimes he took a volume to the Botanic Gardens situated across the Yarra River from Melbourne's main football oval which is built like a Roman stadium. As he lay reading, the human thunder of the barrackers, swelling and dying and rising again, carried across the river to remind him of the roar of the Byzantine factions. He explained this to Stephens:

As to Nika riots—Famous riots between green and blue (not orange) factions in the chariot races at Constantinople in time of Justinian (A.D.532). Mine is the usual spelling in Gibbon and elsewhere e.g. "During fine days Constantinople was abandoned to the factions, whose watchword, Nika, vanquish! has given a name to this memorable sedition"—Gibbon. Omit "quotes" from "Nika," I think.

As to the last verse—Doesn't "whether to" jar more than the manner of "Where? down to"? How would this do?

> Mayhap to Failure's midnight sea
> Or Dawnward? Aye, to God?

I don't like "mayhap" much. It seems a sort of cousin to "eftsoons." Would be glad to hear any news of fate of "pomes." [5]

II. *Three Watchwords*

In "Dawnward?" as we know it from the collected *Poems*, there are four stages of approximation to the position of the last stanza; each "watchword" is examined in turn and found to lack certainty, for, the poet implies, only in attachment to spiritual ideals can Man seek democratic ends. Another section of the letter to Stephens quoted above indicated both O'Dowd's doubt and his use of the "watchwords":

"Reddish"—I prefer to "ruddy." I want a *doubt* to pervade the whole piece. French rougeatre, I am told, is the exact word here to convey my meaning. "Far ahead"—not overhead. Idea is of clouds in the far distance discharging their contents. "Three watchwords" (i.e. Freedom, Equality, Fraternity. 2 verses each). It is thus essential to re-insert the two verses dropped out during previous publication or to recast. As to first "fraternity" verse I had this alternative:

> Subtend the arcs of racial spite
> With bloody clouds of war.

Taking a term from film production, it is possible to analyse the method by means of which the poet has broken up the basic image into a series of significant "shots" or "scenes," viewed, as it were, from different directions, angles, and depths. He might be said to have assembled these in a manner that gives movement to the narrative. Perhaps it is even permissible to speak of the "montage" of the poem. At a later point, in section three, the poem moves away from description to comment and adds appropriate and reinforcing allusions.

The opening scene is a view of distant earth and sky, changing abruptly to a "close-up" of the struggling masses. As they pass, the "fetish" signs inscribed on their flags are seen to be the slogans of the French bourgeois revolution. O'Dowd shows that even if these slogans be accepted as unquestioningly as the magic words of Pallas Athena reflected by "the pantomimic sky" above the "heedless masses," they might well lead to a greater tyranny. In the heavy sky the "sad-eyed mystics" see the "cryptic figures" of Noah's sons, Shem, Ham, and Japheth, and Japheth's son Gog. These represent portion of the table of nations, but O'Dowd uses them to personify Arabia, Africa, Europe, and Asia respectively:[6]

> Prophetic 'mid the whirlwind flow
>   These cryptic figures steal:
> Are they to be for further woe,
>   Or may they be for weal?

The setting for the tableaux is given in the line, "On rushing Cloudland's stage above," clearly drawing attention to the ancient drama-form where, above the human actors, an upper platform rises and upon which appear the superhuman figures. At this point the spatial symbolism all but disappears and the fourth section of the poem refers, with a noticeable mingling of loneliness, pity, and frustration, to some of the events that had occupied O'Dowd's interest as a *Tocsin* journalist: "This is the interpretation of the thing: MENE; God hath numbered thy kingdom, and finished it."[7] The strain and tension is also apparent in the vivid image from physics:

> Will centre-seeking "Culture" hold
>   Tangential Passion's bolt?
> Yield orbits of an Age of Gold,
>   Or comets of Revolt?

III. *Recurring Dreams*

Again, there is the element of descent, and associated with it a sense of futile motion. It is possible, when accepted with the overwhelming idea of a transition from darkness to light, from the pangs of social death to new life, to feel the force of the poet's personal nightmare of "failure's midnight sea." This haunting vision of a dead rotting sea at the bottom of the world to which he drifted with no hope of escape, came to him as an aftermath of an attack of typhus followed by a general breakdown.[8] Also, the recurrent night-dream may be partly interpreted in terms of the myth of a night journey under the sea. In his formulation of this vital process, Jung found that it was associated with a mental or spiritual rebirth. According to his view, the regression takes place when conscious or habitual adaptation fails and frustration is experienced. From a more general viewpoint,[9] the pattern of the rebirth archetype has been seen as typical of the psychological sequence of religious feeling, or frustration, suspended response, followed by a new orientation through the liberation of fantasies and their projection upon the situation that led to the withdrawal. Similarly, in the rebirth archetype the pattern includes a return from the state of corruption, renewed and changed.

In an early contribution to his column, "The Forge," [10] O'Dowd attacked the Victorian squatters, who, when fencing their holdings, had erected gates across the roads adjoining their properties. He later used the same material on the alienation of land as the basis of several articles on land reform. His remarks shed considerable light on his attitude to reform generally. "A jaunt to the country during the holidays" aroused the idea "that reform of any kind without land reform is ultimately worthless." He had seen large tracts of land in the rich Western District of Victoria "devoted to the sustenance and luxury of a few men and their economically worthless and socially frivolous and antidemocratic women folk," while large numbers of "honest poorly-nurtured" people in country towns and Melbourne went hungry. The real importance of the article lies in one paragraph:

Some years later, while travelling on the same [railway] line, I noticed a large board by a wayside railway station containing a large amount of statistics, etc., under the bold legend "Open the Roads and Save the Country." Fellow travellers told me that a crank had erected this board; but knowing that this railway station was a solitary break in a vast squatting demesne, and remembering what my father had told me before [about "dummying" and land rackets], I didn't altogether "cotton" to the crank theory.[11]

This was his second lesson on land reform; others came from the stories told by his father and from his reading. O'Dowd noted particularly the return journey of Tiberius Gracchus through Italy from Spain, when reading Merivale's *Fall of the*

Roman Empire, and considered "that account seemed to give a universal significance to the isolated facts I had noticed myself in Victoria."

IV. *Open the Road!*

The *Tocsin* articles of 1897 and 1898 might seem distant to the post-*Dawnward?* verse. Keeping in mind his general position when that first book appeared, his return to Christianity in 1903, and the affirmation expressed in the poem "Open the Roads," the intervening years had not lessened the value of the material: [12]

> "Open the roads and save our land!"
> The wayside signboard said:
> Squatter's domains on either hand
> Horizonwards were spread.
>
> Seasons of weal and woe have passed;
> No longer it appears
> But with a more than clarion blast
> It thrills me through the years.
>
> "Crank of the track!" the squatters sneered;
> But to my childhood's eyes
> Magical power in the rune appeared,
> And my manhood knows it wise.

The three stanzas quoted set the nominal subject, and the fourth, fifth, and sixth, at a slightly different intensity, seem only to extend this "political" poem on land reform. The juxtaposition of "dawn"—"spark" and "noon"—"flame" is one of the few noticeable points about these particular verses:

> Rune of my dawn you helped to light
> The rebel spark, that soon
> Blazed to a flame for social Right,
> And radiant sails my noon.

The poem as a whole, while superficially pointing to the need for moral and spiritual change, may be interpreted also in terms of ancient poetic myth and ritual in which the symbolism of buried corn plays such a large part. These correspondences go beyond the coloring of the gospel story, and in a very general way "Open the Roads" represents the renewal phase of the night-journey myth. There is certainly a marked change in tone and attitude, and a reflection of this in the flexibility of rhythm and inflection, to the verse written at the end of the nineteenth century:

> Open the road and save our seed
> From reekage of the slums!
> Open the roads, for Landless Need
> With his gaunt battalions comes!
>
> Open the roads and save the land
> From stifling cities' night?
> Open the roads to Learning and
> Wide open them to Light!

V. *The Christian Way*

In the poetic world of Bernard O'Dowd, the wheat-image at last became dynamic and his vision of growth constituted a holy rebirth wherein man participated and found an expression of his own nature. And although O'Dowd was fond of the parable of the tares, in this poem he refers more to the appropriate passage from St. Paul, since it gives the double aspect of the new life won through death and the sense of a life-giving spirit, a supra-personal life within the group.[13]

It is in verse nine that the poem begins to twist away from the merely political:

> Privilege occupies the slopes,
> His suckers choke the wood:
> Homeless below Penury gropes
> For love, for light, for good.

When set beside a typical stanza from a poem written in the late nineties this is quite clear:

> Our pastures had been planted
> With foreign poison weeds:
> With plutocratic dogmas
> Our democratic creeds.
> ("Goodbye Ben!")

Eight years prior to the printing of "Open the Roads," O'Dowd had spoken of destiny as "the road to (?), macadamised by God,"[14] and in verse eleven of this poem demands the construction of "Corduroy tracks that guide to Peace" through "swamps of Pain." The implication is that Christian ideals provide the safest road and, no doubt, carries an allusion to Bunyan's allegory where Pilgrim flees the City of Destruction across the fields and through the gate. "True, there are, by the direction of the Law-giver, certain good and substantial steps placed even through the very midst of this slough; but . . . men, through the dizziness of their heads, step beside, and then they are bemired to purpose, notwithstanding the steps be there." [15]

> We are so burdened with our loads
> We have no time or heart to aspire
> Up to the skies where lead the roads
> Our better selves desire.
>
> Vices degrading in such swarms
> The narrow alley yields,
> Yearn as we may they blur the Forms
> That beckon from the fields:
>
> Open the gates where through we may
> On their holier errands plod!
> Clear all the vicious scrub away,
> And open the road, To God!

O'Dowd's renewed vision of Christianity was an important factor in his later poetic vitality. By itself it could have reduced his creativity, because he saw in Christianity the consummation of his own imaginative life. His sensitivity to the suffering of his fellows was a second factor, and possibly the original impetus in his writing poetry, while a third experience, his love affairs after the break-up of his marriage in 1901, changed completely the manner of his thinking and the direction of his life. Thus, it is not sufficient simply to trace literary, political, and philosophical sources through the maze of O'Dowd's poetic imagery and let these stand as a complete account of the man's thought.

The design of the work written after 1906 is not a result of the effort of conscious thought alone, but is largely determined by forces that lie open only indirectly to thought and the control of the will. The sequence of the "mature" poems presents the movement of spirit; of the paralyzing spell of indecision undone by the impulse of admiration and human love, and of the re-awakening of energies both within and without.

VI. *Priest Unfrocked*

Enter the library of the Victorian Supreme Court in Melbourne and take a seat at the table under the dome. Presently you will notice a tall, slight man who stands at the door of an inner office answering questions. One after another approaches him for advice—where to find a book, where to find the reference to a case, where to look for evidence of a debated legal principle. Students and barristers' clerks —easily, courteously he sets them on the road. Presently he turns; his face is pale, but his hair is rusty black; and he has in his blood the iron of those who strive and endure. Brow and eyes set him apart; he has a scholar's lofty head, the large mild eyes of a dreamer, glowing with the light from within. Bernard O'Dowd is a priest without a frock, a priest devoted not to the service of a creed, but to the service of humanity.[16]

So A. G. Stephens wrote of O'Dowd in 1905. A few years earlier, Stephens had begun issuing small booklets of some of the best verse contributed to the *Bulletin,* and O'Dowd was asked to collect together a selection of his own scattered work. The result was *Dawnward?,* a result achieved in spite of difficulties caused by changes of mind. A biographical note to the volume was disliked by the poet and only the subscribers' copies, fifty in number, were issued with the notes at the back, but lacking the poem "May Day." [17] Another fifty copies, for O'Dowd, contained the poem but omitted the biographical details.

More serious was the confused exchange of telegrams between Stephens and O'Dowd over the "Author's Note" in which he apologized for the tone of a portion of the contents:

As, since writing the verses preceding, the author has returned to Christianity, he cannot help noticing a flippancy of tone inconsistent with that reverence for names and ideas dear to Christians which even in his wanderings in non-Christian realms and wastes of the universe he had wished to preserve. These remarks apply particularly to one line on page 7, one verse on page 10, one line on page 16. And the author trusts that the reader will make the modifications which, owing to the advanced stage of the printing, he himself has been unable to make.[18]

The first instance asked whether the white missionary, Japhet, would continue to lead colored people to the Cross, "with tentacles of his trading greed / and drivel of his Christ?" Page ten spoke of a priesthood celebrating "a diabolic eucharist / with chalices of hate," and that on page sixteen referred to an amoral life-force prizing the lower organisms more highly "than wifeless Christ upon His Cross." Only two copies had been printed when O'Dowd sent a final telegram to Stephens—"omit Author's Note."

VII. *Ideological Drivel*

Dawnward? brought bright new words and fresh imagery to the timid conservatism of Australian poetry, yet the manner of the freshly fledged writer was quite old-fashioned with his rhetorical tone and use of outmoded "poetic" words. "The poetry in *Dawnward?*" O'Dowd's biographers point out, "was rigorous and essentially masculine; the austere stanzas were tight-packed with thought. And this thought was about matters lying uneasily at the bottom of the general mind—on the future of the country, on the dangers ahead of it, on whether it had justification for its democratic faith." Professor Moore[19] wrote of this first book as being "entirely social in nature, dealing with such subjects as democracy, Australia, the city, the press, the proletaria, the outcasts of society, and such kindred topics as time-serving poets, with compromise, hate, and love as expressed in modern society."

Professor Walter Murdoch, writing as Elzevir in the *Argus,* found when considering the book as a whole, *Dawnward?* was "wanting in the radiant serenity of great poetry," but O'Dowd's utterance "has an originality which makes the most hackneyed measure seem like a new poetic form; and his profound sincerity, the fervour of his belief in the capacities of humanity, the intensity of his wrath and his pity—these things emphatically set him with those who, in his own words "Are cleansing for the Harmonist / The City of His Dream." [20]

A third professor, in a recent glance at "the most distinguished of the Austral bards of Progress," attacked his work generally, and no doubt *Dawnward?* in particular, as "a *cloaca maxima* into which has flowed all the ideological drivel of the nineteenth century—deism, pantheism, nationalism, socialism, democratism and the rest—and its value as literature is nil." [21] The view of McAuley is an extreme one; usually O'Dowd's first publication is considered to be "uncommonly stimulating" and "full of leashed force and often moving nobly." [22]

In 1905 A. G. Stephens reprinted *Dawnward?* in a collection named *A Southern Garland* which received a savage reception from an English magazine, *The Academy.* That review was printed in Australia by the *Bulletin* on 9 September, and several weeks later the same newspaper carried the comments of the poets included in *A Southern Garland*. O'Dowd, in his remarks, admitted that the verses in *Dawnward?* "are mainly destructive, destructive of the evil features (if anything is evil) of our bourgeois social system, as 'effete' and dangerous a 'despotism' as ever afflicted man." He went on to give his view of his craft. In O'Dowd's judgment, verse should be assessed by its note of universality, its quality, and the originality of the ideas expressed. "Thought," he stated, "is a more important element in the valuation of absolute poetry than form or melody: form as an end, and melody as an end, have resulted in both local and English sterilization; and originality of thought (i.e., inspiration plus 'essential brain work') must come back to the Muse before she will become fecund of poetry as distinguished from guitar-libretto." [23]

CHAPTER SEVEN

The Ships of Love

THE EXTRA-MARITAL affairs of Bernard O'Dowd have never been openly discussed; most critics of his poetry have completely ignored their existence and, therefore, their importance in understanding the substance of his thought. His biographers give love no more than a timid, sidelong glance. His marriage to Eva, his affair with Constance, and his life with Marie, were experiences that not only affected his outer daily routine but also brought new qualities to his writing. These qualities have been welcomed by many critics without being attributed to anything more than intellectual decision. His ideas and emotions about love, however, inform almost every poem printed after 1904, besides having a marked influence upon portions of the later and longer works.

O'Dowd's concept of love is the only instance of development in his poetry, and the verbal pattern reflects closely the mental and physical, and even moral, changes that took place in the poet between 1889 and 1920. The dates, of course, are merely limiting ones that indicate the period of emotional tumult.

Although he once referred vaguely to an experience that took place about 1885, "which shadowed life since and made me think that I would never seek a mate of my own tribe," it is from the date of his marriage to Evangeline Fryer that it is possible to trace manifestations of his love-life. On November 4, 1889, O'Dowd wrote to Sydney Jephcott to inform him that he had "entered into the gardens of Hymen." He was contented, he said, but without energy and full of "world *ennui*"—"this crying to the spirit of evolution: 'Thou hast made a mistake, all is *not* for the best!'" Many years later he told Nettie Palmer of his "one great affection," but went on to say that it was "not the love that takes one out of one's self."

I. *The Germ of Life*

The years from 1890, when the first son Montaigne was born, were for Mrs. O'Dowd ones necessarily devoted to child-bearing

and the care of her growing family. Rudel was born in 1894 and
followed in 1895 by Auster. Yet another son, Amergin, arrived
three years later. With the birth of Vondel in 1904, the family
of five boys was complete.

O'Dowd's references in verse to sex during these years were
limited to procreation. He has "Cupid" claim that

> My only care is that blind Life
> Shall man the world-ship's deck
> In spite of peace, in spite of strife,
> Until its day of wreck! [1]

"Venus Genetrix," in *Dominions of the Boundary,* is also limited
to a concern that the human race shall increase and multiply:

> Wherever beats the pulse of life
> In rushing Cosmos' plan,
> I am the mother and the wife
> of every god and man.[2]

A period of acute emotional conflict began in 1900 due to
O'Dowd's relationship with Constance H———. She was, the
poet said, "someone that lit me," but the impulses that illuminated his being were against the Catholic conception of morality
with which he had grown up. The struggle to remain true to
his ethical standard and his wife went on for three years, until
the woman left the country. Although the crisis was not religious
in origin, it had the effect of causing a temporary return to the
Catholic Church.

Constance, as O'Dowd remembered her, "was a big-souled being worthy of being sought through Time, Space, Heaven and
other places, but the crisis had passed during her absence." She
"dowered" his "vigour with a second youth" and inspired large
quantities of rather banal verse, most of which was suppressed
by the poet. Two "manuscript" poems did, however, reach print
in Stevens' *Anthology of Australian Verse* (1906). The first was
entitled "Love's Substitute" and shows a simple extension of his
previous thoughts:

> Sour social soils untilled need Love's own nerve
> That Pence-a-flower may oust their weedy hates:
> And till the Wolves of Want abate their ruth
> The perfect lover's symbol is "We Serve!"

O'Dowd's second contribution to the collection reiterates again
"Our Duty":

"Yet what were Love . . . / If thought is chained, and gagged
is Speech and lies / Enthroned as Law befoul posterity."

His love sometimes took on the aspect of a ship's captain, steer-
ing the vessel through "darkly-whirling maelstroms of the mind"
to "the calm where Love's High Lights we may pursue":

> I know not quite the bearings of your goal,
> Its voyage's compass, currents of its charts,
> Nor how unaided 'mid such waves to plough,
> But you are good, and Highest Good imparts
> His own unerring sight to each brave prow
> That threads, for good, these seaways of the soul.
>
> (17 December 1905)

She was also a bird, pursued and pursuing:

> Nor deem the singer vain for well he knows
> There also was a secret contest run
> When he was willing quarry to your skill
> And you the kestrel amorous to fill
> His quivering being with the glory-glow
> That make the kestrel and the quarry one.
>
> (9 March 1906)

Yet he knew

> Altho' 'tis meet these kestrel unions be,
> Since future skies their shepherds thus obtain,
> A moment's right may not be daylong joy
> For those equipped with prescient eyes and brain,
> And we are winged, the raider to destroy,
> The sad to succour and the bond to free.
>
> (9 March 1906)

II. *The Tide of Love*

One poem, "Love and Sacrifice," written in 1903 under Constance's influence is full of challenge and exultation.[3] As H. M.
Green says, it is a "fine, though rather too long poem" written
in a new meter of a rhymed quatrain in four even lines (6:6:6:6)
as against the long-preferred "fourteener" (8:6:8:6).[4]

> Can we not consecrate
> To man and God above
> This volume of our great
> Supernal tide of love?

the poet asks. When "the world is full of woe" and "modern baseness," such love is wasted on one couple who should sacrifice their "repose in rosy bower":

> If sacrifice may move
>   Their load of pain from men
> The greatest right of Love
>   Is to renounce It then.
>
> Ah, Love, the earth is woe's
>   And sadly helpers needs:
> And, till its burden goes,
>   Our work is where it bleeds.

The lady passed out of his life forever, leaving behind a randy poet and a tormented wife and mother. O'Dowd characteristically, and calmly, described the effect on himself: "The effort to keep Venus Urania on a cold pedestal and to ignore that she was one eternally with Venus Pandemos failed, and as a result, I came back to my fellows on this earth again saddened perhaps but rendered more wholesome, better, and wiser by my memories of Astralia."

He "came back," but convinced there was no basis for "forcing the supreme affection" for his wife; believing, in fact, that it had never existed. That he was "more wholesome, better, and wiser" is open to question.

He "hungered" for "Eternal Venus" though "churlish seas forbade one ever hold / Her hand in mine again"—until he met poetess Marie Pitt: "Another guiding star appeared upon the blue / To me sad summer day when she returned / With all the gifts that I had hungered for." (2 April 1915.) Mrs. O'Dowd, having reached the verge of nervous breakdown, consulted a lawyer. Bernard left the house to take lodgings with Mrs. Pitt at Merri. In 1924 the pair moved to 155 Clarke Street, Northcote; to the bleak, two-storey brick house where he died in 1953.

Several years after leaving his wife and children, the poet, who was also Victoria's Parliamentary Draughtsman, was still speaking of his "sense of duty to Mrs. O'Dowd" and his anxiety to avoid causing her pain. This alone had prevented his leaving "years ago"!

Desert islands pall after a few years experience of them and man is a weary being if always alone. I'd like to be thought heroic, I suppose, to my friends, but I'd filled the lonely role for thirty years or so and—well the heroism collapsed—and, saving always the thought of the sufferings of Mrs. O'Dowd, very terrible, very real and very undeserved, I am very glad it did collapse. But it's very hard not to see one's boys when one loves them.

III. I, Me, and Mine

Bernard O'Dowd appears to have gone through several stages in his search for a unity and stability of outlook and endeavour. The volcanic eruptions of emotion that shattered the domestic crust in 1900 produced a man self-haunted by his relations with Her and by the image of himself loving. Nevertheless, love must be sacrificed to the world's ills. By 1907, when the poet was apostrophizing "Sappho," he had approached the view "that the most potent solvents of wrong, tyrannies, castes, classes, . . . are not the nitric apostrophes to gods of destruction, but songs of love for one another." [5] The verses in his collected *Poems* following *The Seven Deadly Sins*, and titled "Miscellaneous," are mostly "battle songs" of love addressed to Marie Pitt:

> I know that I am also you,
>   That you are I, that all are we;
> Time nor space can our love disperse;
>   We are the captain and the crew,
> Never the tempest we shall rue. . . .

We notice in these poems how the writer slowly sublimated his human love into the love of wisdom and the love of God, until finally, he transcended and universalized the object of his affection in a theory of all-pervading love. Love became the panacea: "Love is such a veritable potency woven with the structure of the universe that even physical changes for the better are more easily possible for its properly tapped and properly directed energies than any Caesars, Napoleons, or ideal constitution could ever bring about." [6]

In a delightful simmer of creative joy that he felt was the poetic counterpart of love, O'Dowd realized that "persons cease to be individual altogether, they actually *become* universal types, both the 'I' and the 'you.' One seems to get into regions where there are no individuals because they are all (in one)." [7]

"An occasional luxury of mine," O'Dowd wrote to the *Bulletin's* "Red Page" editor in 1910, "is to weave fancies of all kinds around the theme of Ferdinand and Miranda. While at this lately

I was thinking of the platonic and mystic idea of the divided parts of the one soul seeking each other through the world and ages until success and consequent merging, away from earth, into one angel." [8] To this strange idea he added the remarkable one of the descent of the soul into matter and its subsequent reascension, and attempted to find a poetic form to symbolize the combination.

IV. *Icy Gnostic Spells*

The invention of the "Mirandelay" came after many sheets of writing paper had been used in a mess of false starts and word-hints. The form combines the characteristics of the glose and the reversolet. A glose has verses ending in the consecutive lines of the first verse and McKay's reversolet, O'Dowd considered, "was the very thing to express in form the descent and ascent of the soul." The verses might be numbered—

$$1\ 2\ 3\ 4\ 5\ 6\ /\ 2\ 3\ 4\ 5\ /\ 6\ 5\ 4\ 3\ 2\ 1$$

where the middle section, or "waist," consists of five verses each beginning with a line from the first verse and the final verse is simply the first in reverse order of lines:

> Soul I would with mine one angel form
> Mind I roam with on the stellar way
> Heart I throb with when the weary moan
> Eyes unfathomed that light my own
> Smile serene that smooths the creased days
> Sylph of paradise, yet woman warm.

The numerous first drafts were all written on October 1, 1910, and put aside for a week. He then finalized his corrections and revisions, and the next day sent the completed poem to the *Bulletin*. Together with the poem and O'Dowd's comment, the editor of the "Red Page" issued a challenge to readers to try their ability in a Mirandelay competition. The resulting entries were of a uniformly low standard.[9]

Objecting violently and crying "O Tempora! O Mores!! O'Dowd!!!," H. C. McKay, who was said to be the inventor of the reversolet, wrote to the newspaper.[10] Emerging from a seance, McKay said, "there fluttered toward me out of the ether a slip of faded paper. I seized it eagerly. It proved to be an unpaid laundry-bill, on the back of which was scribbled in a hand tremulous and shaky from inexpressible emotion":

By the mouldy Melbourne law-courts, lookin' sideways to the sea
There's a frenzied bard a-settin', and I know he thinks o' me:
For the Norms are in his brain cells an' the tramcar-bells, they say,
'Shape a dream, O Keltic hormone, shape a mild Mirandelay—
  Shape a mild Mirandelay
  Where the co-respondents stray—
Can't you hear the lawyers gloatin' o'er your weird Mirandelay?
  On the road to M'randelay
  Where the flying adverbs play,
An' O'Dowd comes up in wonder out o' Chaos, 'crost the Bay!'

This amusing though obvious parody of Kipling sets out Mc-
Kay's grounds for criticizing the new form. First, he did not
consider O'Dowd's Mirandelay to be a legitimate combination
of the reversolet and glose at all, but a bastard variation:

I seen 'im first a-dreamin' with an index by his side,
A Reversolet ('e pinched it) an' a Glose wot nearly died,
An' 'e wed 'em (in 'is brain-cells) in the Christian Science way—
An' their orfspring was an 'arf-caste, which 'e called 'Mirandelay'.

His second criticism had more validity. "Such a form is ... essentially limiting and artificial, owing to the monotony of the
repetition." The *Bulletin,* however, said the last word in defence
of O'Dowd. "The mirandelay," the editor wrote, "may not be
the best possible combination of the glose and the reversolet,
but it is O'Dowd's mirandelay."

What O'Dowd thought is not known, but he omitted "Mirandelay" from any collections of his verse. In fact, suppression was
the fate of the bulk of his writing inspired by his love affairs.
There are reminiscent passages in some later poems, such as:

    There was a time
  When gods spun daily marvels for my boon,
   And let my mortal ears forget their bars
  And overhear the sempiternal rune
   Of lunar base and great contralto stars,
    And cleansed the rime
  Out of mine eyes till they beheld a noon,

from "An Ode to Sydney," and several portions of "The Bush"
celebrate "the human symbol of that Love":

   My old ideals She would tune until
    The grating note of self no longer rang:
   She drove the birds of gloom and evil will
    Out of the cote wherein my poems sang.

CHAPTER EIGHT

Slave of the Striking Word

ADMIRERS of O'Dowd's poetry consider that *The Silent Land,* "came, as if on a fresh wind, from a new direction." [1] He wrote, to continue the metaphor, with gentler emotion and less force but the chill air bit deeper. This series of poems refers to an idea somewhat similar to Emerson's Oversoul, the "many-celled abode" of mankind:

> Is there behind all men that live
> One all-containing Soul,
> Whose symbols, apt for each one, give
> A transcript of the whole?

Again, it is that Unity "within which every man's particular being is contained and made one with all other" (Emerson); it is a mystic world where past and present, the living and the dead, are merged:

> All men live here, but know it not,
> Wise, foolish, leader, led,
> The saint, the sinner, and the sot—
> The living and the dead.

And further, all contribute in acts and thoughts. Whether for good or for evil, no vibrations are lost but are stored in this Oversoul to influence mankind:

> That where a wrong is done to men,
> Whate'er their race or birth,
> The wound is felt, again, again,
> By every man on earth.

The poet transfers to *The Silent Land* something akin to the doctrine of the conservation of energy and gives physical immortality to every thought and emotion of the ages. Lost dreams, lost deeds are the shadowy limbo of this domain which many readers will equate with the world of the subconscious mind;

73

the Other World that is everywhere in us and around us, never seen, seldom recognized, but felt perpetually. Today it might properly be termed the "collective subconscious" mind.

In this context it is not strange to note that the collected poems of the Canadian poet, Wilfred Campbell, duplicate O'Dowd's mind and motive. "Soul" imitates the philosophy of *The Silent Land*, and "Genius" approaches so closely to O'Dowd it is difficult to distinguish thought from thought. Both books were published at roughly the same time!

Among Bernard O'Dowd's literary papers was a notebook that contained jottings indicating the way in which he intended mapping the regions of *The Silent Land*. "Topography of SL. Fas. Gods. The Young the good ones. The poor. The Silent Churches Temples. Revolts. The lighted ranges of Love. The awful Tales of love. Duty. Prayer. Lords. Boundaries." Comparison with the book shows that while most of these subjects were touched on, the final order was changed. The group making up *The Silent Land* was written between 1904 and 1905 and read, in part, to the November 1905 meeting of the Literature Society of Melbourne. "Quail" was written during the Autumn of 1905 and "Fallow" and "Fas" a little later in that same year. "Love and Sacrifice," although composed as early as 1903, was not printed until 1905.

I. *Light Beyond the Atmosphere*

When the second edition of *The Silent Land* was published in 1909, O'Dowd found it "queer fun" to read. "I've scarcely looked at it as a whole since first publication," he wrote to Nettie Palmer, "and so I could read it with some aloofness—the feeling of amused tolerance towards much of it that I wrote with well-remembered deadly seriousness, was a particularly healthy experience. Anyhow, I like it myself now in a sort of unbiassed way and am glad the fellow wrote it." [2]

It is a book of poetry with a greater range than *Dawnward?*, with the variations on its central theme more universal than social. Nevertheless, there is a quantity of flat explanatory matter in it and individual poems are marred in places by a rigidity of language which reads, as someone said, like a paraphrase of Mental Science publications. There are such headstrong contemporary images as the influences that "Lead Inspiration's conduit pipes / From Higher Waterfalls" and many prosaic lines: "Such glows reflected from the world / As almost to illume."

The *Bulletin,* in a "Poet of the Moment" item, gave O'Dowd's recreation as "hunting the big, bounding Word through the trackless thesaurus." [3] His bag certainly contains the raw meat of polysyllabic jargon, and within lines of each other one is likely to come face to face with "psychopomp," "protplast," and "autochthonic." He is very well read, one reviewer commented, but "the pity of it is he is so disposed to empty the results of his reading on the counter." [4]

On the positive side, *The Silent Land* contains many passages of taut dignity and several haunting verses:

> With no small compass in His blue
> Did God our circle plot,
> For man may do what he dare do,
> Except what He would not.

There are lines of good poetry, good philosophy, and good humanity:

> We are not all the Self we seem;
> We are twined around with men
> Who once performed this mortal dream,
> And dream in us again.

There is movement in the lines where the poet strives to catch echoes of invisible forces and affirms:

> Yea, they were great, and are, and while
> Earth's forces last, will be:
> Their Silent frown, their Silent smile
> Deflects our destiny.

But more than this, there are flashes of imagery that give life even to commonplace stanzas: "They give us lamps till tempest lifts, / St. Elmos of our dark," and "Antipodean Prosperos, Mirandas of the South"; or the emergence from the subconscious of "Great portents of the sunny noon / That make the reckless wise."

Although *The Silent Land* was an augury of the future O'Dowd, he remained generally cramped by the crustacean stanza he had chosen—a regal 4:3 iambic quatrain with alternating rhymes. The regularity of this monotonous meter was varied by long and short lines:

> 'Tis woven with the world we hear,
>   In subtlest tapestry:
> Our sounds are but translations clear
>   Of its dumb symbolry.

In the above instance, however, he has used two weak end-
rhymes where one would have given sufficient relief; in "Threshold Murmurs," he weakened his usually masculine verse in en-
deavouring to vary his melody with too many trivial words and
jarring articles:

> Our half-felt sighs some tale tell true
>   Of the Silent Land's romance,
> Of the Silent Me and the Silent You,
>   Enamoured or askance.

II. *The Abiding Gods*

Poetry Militant, O'Dowd's prose justification of his own practice, calls upon poets the function of creating gods, "and in
every age of human progress the poet has been the most authen-
tic and effective creator of gods and of the mythologies that
give bone and blood and power." In this particular instance, at
least, O'Dowd might be said to have gained control of the market
in seasoned, pedigreed gods: his imagination grasped the special
power and function of each one of the old universal forces, but
his superiority caused Inglis Moore to remark—"O'Dowd has the
true Emersonian touch, and both transcendentalists wear an air
of patronising self-importance, inspired, not unnaturally, by the
consciousness that they—and they alone—have been granted the
Secret and the Revelation." [5]

As a mystic, the poet hears the mysterious voices of *The Silent
Land*. The theme of "The Gods" in that book sketches what became, a year later, the subject of *Dominions of the Boundary;*
the Powers (gods) from the boundary between this world and
the next, between the known and unknown. [6] This last-mentioned
book is often said to concern the "old gods brought up-to-date."
"The title does not refer to places—persons are meant—names
of an order in the old hierarchy of angels, and are used to represent the powers that seem to govern the regions on the boundary
of the seen and unseen." [7] In this view, "Vulcan" is equated
with industry, "Earth" with instinct, "Sirens" the charms of
women, "Juno" motherhood, and "Isis" equals spiritual wisdom.

Certainly, there is a note in O'Dowd's script to the effect that Juno represents the earth Spirit, fertility; that "Mnemosyne" is memory of past error and a stimulus to prevention and mutation, and the "Winds" are "forces that make for or effect, or deflect, civilisation." And certainly Dominions or Dominations are one of the choirs in the ranks of the celestial spirits, and O'Dowd does use the ancient names as titles for individual poems. But he certainly did not confine himself to a theism of eternal attributes. While he illuminated the old symbolism of the gods, he also high-lighted their contemporary significance. As Professor Walter Murdoch wrote: "Mr. O'Dowd is not retelling a set of stories from the Greek mythology; he is writing, not about dead gods, but about—his old subject—the living forces by which human life is guided and controlled; forces which, however the names men know them by may pass and be forgotten, are themselves eternal and unchangeable." [8]

The substance of *The Silent Land* and *Dominions of the Boundary*, as Frederick Macartney points out, is more metaphysical than *Dawnward?* and less strident in tone; "the thought and the music," in Moore's opinion, "have gained a fresh fluency and directness of expression." [9] Henry Green, in his *History of Australian Literature*, also finds more than promise in these volumes of poetry:

Naive, arid, monotonous as they are, there is yet something compelling about them; the poet's fervent but austere conviction warms them with a dry fire; they are coloured by an originality that belongs not to the ideas they convey but to the breadth and depth of his realization of those ideas: they are instinct with power; they make it clear that a new and strikingly individual poetic personality has appeared.[10]

III. *Vast Formless Things*

O'Dowd's brief, to employ legal terminology, is outlined in the three quotations prefacing *Dominions of the Boundary*. Colossians states "all things were created by Him and for Him," Edgar Allan Poe indicates the "Vast formless things / That shift the scenery to and fro," while William Blake hints darkly at "divine names, which, when erected into gods, become destructive to humanity." In short, the old gods are the personification of the Omnipotent under some one of His many aspects.

The gods were once realities, O'Dowd says, and are influences today:

> But tho' we mumble sceptic saw,
>   Or sweet old prayers forget;
> And tho' we dream of Higher Law,
>   The gods are living yet.

"No monitor"—no superstition—will they allow save that of one unknown, the fear of something behind things. All the gods are avowed by thoughts and deeds, not by any "cult of names" or "pattering of creeds," but active belief in the ancient gods was swept away in the Middle Ages:

> When mediaeval hurricane
>   The gods in exile drove,
> "Thrice-greatest" Hermes and his train
>   Usurped the seats of Jove.[11]

Jove, Jupiter, or Zeus, the greatest of the gods, the supreme ruler, was usurped by his son, the messenger of the gods, and the bringer of dreams and refreshing sleep. Mercury, or Hermes, was originally the Power that brought good fortune to men, but he was also the god of ready speech, to which he added cunning, fraud, and even perjury. Today, he offers

> Suburban Delphis for the rich,
>   The Gnosis for the staid!
> Perennial by the road, the witch
>   Of Endor plies her trade! [12]

Although he deals in fortune-telling and Gnostic doctrines for the respectable, the gypsies ("witch of Endor") can still call up the emanations of God, as in centuries past Saul had the woman at Endor "divine" to him "the familiar spirit" of Samuel.[13]

O'Dowd's view of "Hermes" was derived from his research into the occult and the psychic. Trance states, automatic writing, and the rest, led him to believe in Hermes planting the seeds of the "mystical fruit and radiant flowers" of vision and prescience:

> My white magicians ope the skies,
>   My black the vortex plumb;
> Yea, both have warrant in my eyes,
>   And from my kingdom come:
>
> For small in curved immensity
>   The dimly pencilled arc
> Of good or bad, subtended by
>   Your chord of Light or Dark.

None of the gods has fixed forms, O'Dowd reminds his readers in "Heracleitic," but flow constantly from one into another in response to changing currents of Time. Heracleitus, a philosopher of the Ionian school, propounded the theory of constant flux, with the passage of everything backwards and forwards resulting in the harmony of nature—"no man," he wrote, "can twice enter the same river." The poet agrees:

> Life is a stream: through a gorge we go
> 'Tween a deep and a living deep:
> Form is the gorge, and change is the flow,
> And the source and the mouth are sleep.[14]

IV. *Words as Big as Bulls*

Dominions of the Boundary, O'Dowd's third book, "does not differ from his former books, and the stanza is the same, and the big scientific words show no sign of abating, or the capitals of slipping surreptitiously into the lower case, or the neat definitions of becoming any more final." [15] The reviewer could, however, find a suggestion of a theme, a philosophy. "O'Dowd," The *Bulletin* claimed, "is doubtful of the value of the science he has so laboriously studied. Accurately and almost automatically reflecting the present attitude of science, which, having proved that matter does not exist except as a form of motion, now leans toward mysticism, O'Dowd, Science's faithful scribe, begins to doubt the scope and finality of this new knowledge."

Yet even this critic realizes there is more to the book than compact little rime-coated couplets giving precise definitions of Fate and History in the terminology of Science. There is something more, "some hinterland of the senses where strange things may yet wander, some shadowy place whose mysterious twilight may shelter—let us imagine—a soul?" The writer sees a little of O'Dowd's vision of living gods, of a world still plastic to the touch of inspiration, and of windows of the soul not closed to the vagrant winds of wonder.

Dominions contains the most confident work by Bernard O'Dowd in his so-called "fourteener" style; several of the poems in this book are very subtle, some are shaped and glowing with personal feeling, all are intensely serious and positive in statement:

> All is not daylight in the day,
> Or knowledge in the known;

> The life we are, the prayer we pray,
> From deep, to deep, is blown.[16]

Most readers will agree that these poems are compactly phrased, that evidence of wide reading and vocabulary is shown, that O'Dowd is apt at a definition, picturesque and forcible with phrases, but— He recalls the character Euripedes in Aristophanes' "Frogs," who said his method was first of all to produce some scenic effect to attract the attention of his audience, and then "he would speak a dozen words as big as bulls, with crests and shaggy eyebrows." O'Dowd, too, is profusely decorated with big uncouth prosaic terms; he is a slave to the striking word. He flounders, at times, into cheerful jingles that are unconsciously humorous:

> And he who boards my lithe canoe
> And paddles away with me
> Shall land anon on Mount Meru
> And all the Devas see.

He is so economical in words that he makes two-word lines needing a paragraph of explanation—

"Clairaudient interpreter, / Clairvoyant Pythoness—" and even achieves a remarkable feat of compression, a one-word line— "Amanuensis-annalist." But wilful as these faults are, he can break the seemingly inevitable three-beat lines by a sudden change of emphasis:

"And the Winds are his wands," or "Slowly fashioned the world," or "Grapple and wrestle the arrogant Past / All night, until the Dawn!"

V. *The Lapping Higher Tide*

Athene, in ancient myth, personified the guiding influence of life, of wise counsel in industry and in strategy of war. She was the goddess of wisdom and the owl her sacred bird. O'Dowd's "Athena" is a combination of Nordic and Cretan mythology, a mingling of the animal and spiritual. She represents the ideal rationalist: "The truth my worshippers record / For its pure sake alone." Nothing but truth is her concern, and therefore, she is wisdom more than thought. Nevertheless, this Power is overshadowed by one far greater than she:

> Yet I but rule while I obey,
>   For Thought, my region wide,
> Is a dim atoll, wet with the spray
>   Of a lapping Higher Tide.[17]

The poem in the collected edition includes seven stanzas not in the separate publication of *Dominions*, from verses twelve to eighteen inclusive.

Dionysus was the nature god and in general the god of fruitfulness. O'Dowd names his reincarnation Bacchus, the Power of lofty enthusiasm:

> I am the gift of tongues that flame
>   Inspired resolve above:
> I wither the woods of paltry aim
>   That choke the growth of love.

The poet is anxious to disassociate his god from the usual idea of the self-indulgent Bacchus. It was Bacchus who glowed in Savonarola's grim words, who raged in Tolstoi, cherished St. Francis, and shone brightly from Nietzsche's eyes:

> All that in love ye cannot buy,
>   In genius baffling prayer,
> In Art beyond the measuring eye,
>   Is immanent Bacchus there.

And it is the spirit of Bacchus which will enable man to quench the fires of hell, raze the walls of Babylon and build man's New Jerusalem:

> And then you know that here below
>   All men so twine with you,
> That he who strikes receives the blow
>   Upon his own face too!
>
> That one man's sin is all men's sin,
>   That love in one saves all:
> That each and all one heaven win,
>   Or to one oblivion fall! [18]

CHAPTER NINE

Poetry Militant

IT HAS been said that Bernard O'Dowd "rationalized his own practice into a theory of poetry"; that first came his need or purpose and then verse to satisfy it.[1] The reference made is to the poet's expressed view of *Poetry Militant*, but the specific application of the "theory" is mostly unwarranted.[2]

The ideal of contemporary life, O'Dowd considered, is commercialism, and the mass of the people, enjoying for the first time the taste of prosperity, tended to follow pleasure for pleasure's sake. Under these circumstances, one of the functions of the lover of literature is to restate, with "fanatical emphasis if necessary, the claims of the intellectual and spiritual powers of the mind to due consideration." All else follows from this basic idea. He must stress the importance of the calling of the literary man in society, examine "theories of artistic conduct," and summon those "fitted to assume the robes and strike the high harp of that calling."

While the power of the theologian wanes and new, "more superficially rational" dogmas grip human minds the poet, as the interpreter of the people, grows more important. He makes science and philosophy "emotionally digestible" to them, and awakens the sense of the wrongs they endure or inflict. The creative poet, however, is not just a "verbal tickler of jaded ears," he is the Baptist of his epoch: "He said, I am the voice of one crying in the wilderness, Make straight the way of the Lord, as said the prophet Esaias."[3] O'Dowd's utilitarian conception of poetry digesting science caused Inglis Moore to complain irritably that he "need not always be incessantly squatting down, like a Polynesian woman, masticating philosophic and scientific roots to turn them into acceptable *kava* for the delectation of the masses."[4]

Continuing to urge the necessity of the useful in art, O'Dowd characterized the poet as the Answerer of real questions. Many since have turned the title about and said O'Dowd was not an answerer, but an asker of questions. And what are these real questions of the age?—the subjects in which people are in-

tensely interested, politics, religion, science, sex and social reform. This statement was immediately applied to O'Dowd's own
work and, as late as 1955, the prophet-without-honor was having it thrown in his face: "When he says in *Poetry Militant* that
politics, religion, sex, science and social reform ... are worthy
subjects of great poetry, one does not imagine that he would
attempt a poem on sex or religion. But that in fact is precisely
what he does, however he calls his poem 'Cupid' or 'Juno' or
'Isis.' He does not write of political *things* or scientific *ideas*—
but simply of Politics and Science." [5]

I. *An Artist's Creed*

O'Dowd took the title of his exposition by analogy from ec-
clesiastical literature, where the function of the Church is marked
by the militant and triumphant stages, and applied it to poetry.
However, fourteen years before he had put forward the same
notion when dealing with "the religion of Spiritualism," claiming
the movement showed too much of the Spiritual Triumphant
idea and too little of the Militant: "The Spiritualist must become
a politician, and do what he can in this region ... to make Man's
lot more bearable. He must work for the oppressed, the sick
and the miserable by means of the ordinary organizations he
finds to hand, and by new and better ones when he can. He must
take sides, and fight hard for the rights of men, of women, of
children, of animals, of inanimate (if there is such) nature." [6]
Although modified over the years, in essentials the creed of
O'Dowd remained the same.[7]

In 1907, two years before *Poetry Militant*, O'Dowd indicated
clearly the trend of his thoughts:

I see signs lately in Australia . . . that men are beginning to find out
that, in poetry, form without matter is dead, and that the poet who
is not essentially a prophet, and with an original foreword to hand his
generation, is certainly not alive enough to stir his audiences into acceptance of the poetic art or craft as a real living thing.[8]

And, in 1942, during a Pleasant Sunday Afternoon address at
Wesley Church, Melbourne, he strongly reiterated his view of
the poet's place in the community:

We want the poet as a prophet to carry a torch among the denizens
of the feudal cobwebs that hang about our halls and to burn us into
flaming hate of the luxuries and the dirty ideals that are weakening

our fibre and preparing us for social and individual serfdom. We want him as advance-guardsman of liberty to rouse us from a political apathy which will tempt the briber and corrupters to operate upon us, and which will, as it has done in the case of other free peoples, times without number, hand us over to the mercies of military despotism, or even worse plutocratic dictatorship.[9]

This call to poets, repeated so many times and in so many ways, was the crux of *Poetry Militant*. The details, over which critics have quibbled ever since, all follow on his distinction between poetry militant and poetry for poetry's sake, which is "the final flower of the human intellect." As the end in view in the militant stage is the "furtherance of the best interest of the human race," "poetry should not bloom merely for the sake of blooming, but for the sake of producing seed." O'Dowd's address is therefore concerned with standards of artistic conduct.

II. *Poetry by Prescription*

Poetry Militant was quickly interpreted as a defense of propaganda verse; poetry, O'Dowd was told, cannot be written to a prescription and must preach indirectly.[10] As for poetry blooming to produce seed, the *Bulletin* reviewer remarked, a rose once blossomed in verse blooms for ever. The claim that poetry must be interesting besides being useful and beautiful was denied in the question—is not beauty in itself interesting? O'Dowd waited thirty-four years before answering these criticisms in an address, "A Little Sister of Religion," delivered in 1943. "The poetry with which materialism is to be fought", he said, "is not necessarily deliberately propagandist verse," but may be such delicate lyrics as Shaw Neilson's "The Orange Tree" or Wordsworth's "Primrose by the River's Brim." "Such suggestive images, deftly presented to young or ardent minds, may make those minds veritable bastions or strong points against the advance of antichrist."

Poetry in 1909 was "saying nothing in a multitude of beautiful words, phrases and forms"; in 1943, "recent poetry" was just as narrow in scope, and "instead of making all life its province, limits its activities to the margins of life—the borderland of the known and unknown, the shadowland between the seen and unseen, the no man's land separating life from death!"

The principal duty of the poet he contended, is to line up and battle "with his subtly powerful methods, for the just and merciful ordering of the world." Poetry must express all feelings of people, the hopes, anxieties and fears so that hope will hearten them to nobler endeavour, anxiety will fade away, and anguish will be assuaged. But poetry should also inflame against injustice, steel against the temptation to take the easy but wrong path, and entrench determination to treat every man as an end in himself. "And the poet will do these things not by the crude methods of the roadside political candidate, but by the lyrical power, or the ballad making power, or the symbolizing power God has given him, or by the allegorical deftness of an Edmund Spencer or John Bunyan, or the miraculous homeliness of the poet Christ in the parables." [11]

III. *An Intellectual Chanter*

In the stage of Poetry Militant men will need new gods to lead them onward, "that is to say, we need embodied principles of action better than our average selves to lead us out of our average selves on to the realization of higher selves," and poets are the most effective creators of gods and their mythologies. This they do by the use of personification, "the first right of the poet, the original tool of the poet." Claiming it as an essential part of his poetic method, O'Dowd made a vigorous defense of personification, demanding that it should be released from the ban imposed on it after Alexander Pope's time, and restored to its rightful place in practice. Of course, any personification must be more than merely assertive capital letters and ugly words; it must have freshness, and blood and sinews and bones.

Closely related to his use of personification is the aim of the images that "lie so thick upon the page that the austere taste of our period is shocked," which is to give concreteness to the abstractions. According to this intellectual purpose an image is a good one when "it conveys the thought with ingenious precision."

Similarly, the equipment of the "Permeator poet" must include a mastery of rhetoric, "good rhetoric, honest moving eloquence, should again become, as it has been throughout all the ages, a legitimate constituent of poetry, nay I would say an absolutely necessary constituent of great poetry." True rhetoric, according to O'Dowd, is the art of "persuading us to adopt the good life individually, socially and internationally." Properly used it enkindles the minds and souls of the people to high aspirations and

plays a large part, with religion and ethical philosophy, in form-
ing and developing a conscience for the people.

While *Poetry Militant* explicitly expresses his conception of
the modern poet's function, it has been used generally as a means
of explaining aspects of O'Dowd's own technique. Inglis Moore
finds *Poetry Militant* vital to both an understanding and an
evaluation of the poetry,[12] and Henry Green, while believing the
gospel to be out-dated, considers O'Dowd's practice accords
closely with his precepts. Thus, when the poet calls for an extreme simplicity of form and finds this in "the fourteen-syllabled
line of Anglo-Saxon and early English poetry," which "subor-
dinates the call of the verbal music to the more important call
of the thought-motif and the spiritual theme," the critics cry
as one, "monotonous!"

"This early work is full of matter, but lacks sap; it is dry,
stringy, monotonous; a long chain of not always very closely related statements which seldom lead anywhere and are delivered
with the monotonous beat of a metronome."[13] Todd also considers that an unwarranted confidence is displayed in the "fourteener," and "the drumming of seven iambic feet constantly repeated needs to be subdued if an impression of the most awful
monotony is to be avoided."[14] Even his younger friend, Frederick Macartney, joined the chorus of academic critics:

The form undoubtedly becomes monotonous though almost hypnotic
in O'Dowd's persistence with it, and objections to that effect led him
to admit in the end that he had perhaps kept it up too long. He chose
it for its tightness and made it tighter by his method of compressing
his meaning, and jammed it too often with polysyllabic words. This
was not for lack of appreciation of technical niceties. He quickly
noticed and would helpfully point out defects marring verse put
before him for an opinion. The only explanation seems to be his
dominating purposiveness. He deafened himself hammering his ideas
solid.[15]

The most recent writer on O'Dowd, A. A. Phillips, when introducing a selection of poetry, offered what is perhaps the clear-
est explanation of the reason behind the poet's use of a deliberately "bare" style. He finds the fervent belief that mankind
can create social structures by willing them, to be the basis of
O'Dowd's idea of the role of the poet. The poet "must not merely
declare the true vision of the destiny of men; he must summon
their will to the achievement of that destiny. To do this, he must
infest them with the intensity of his own conviction."[16]

IV. *Solid Abstractions*

Phillips' statement does not greatly differ from that of Walter Murdoch who, when introducing O'Dowd's collected edition of 1941, said: "His verse had an austere simplicity of form, a classical severity, a lean athletic kind of beauty new to our country's literature. This plain bare style of his was no accident, but the deliberate choice of a poet who had pondered long on the question, what form was best suited to be the vehicle of the message he had to deliver."

The Puritanical purposiveness of the poet led him to adopt the ballad-meter and a strict rhyme-scheme that amounted to an appalling burden. "He was," continues Phillips, "writing intellectual poetry, and setting out to express ideas with a direct accuracy and without sensuous ornament. To do this and simultaneously to find a rhyme on an average of once every seven syllables is an immensely difficult task—and O'Dowd certainly did not successfully achieve it." [17] Ironically, O'Dowd's rhyming is rarely mentioned by reviewers and critics of his work; they prefer to attack the unfashionable and naive aspects such as personification and meter.

O'Dowd, in *Poetry Militant*, found contemporary Australian poetry "singularly barren in original idea, in traces of original thought" and this poverty of modern poetry in general caused him to insist on the duty of the poet to be original and return his own version of the regions given him to explore. But many subjects were taboo in poetry, and a good deal that was interesting and important to humanity at large lay outside the rules. "Too many men of great poetic capacity," O'Dowd considered, "... persist in refusing to deal with great subjects in which the people are intensely interested." There are very few great political poems, and scarcely any great religious or devotional poems. Bluffed by the catch-cry "didactic" the poet will not illumine and humanize science with his poetry, and "as to songs of the relations of the sexes, most poets stop at the commonplaces of traditional sentimentalism, and the staging of unreal thoughts and unfelt feelings."

V. *The Irresistible Intonation*

Both Murdoch and Phillips see O'Dowd in his correct setting. Murdoch tells present-day readers how this "new Australian singer" struck a note in verse for those "tired of the race-course in Australian poetry," and weary of the jingle; "weary, too, of second-hand poetic ornaments made in England." Phillips places O'Dowd in a period when the folk-feeling of the bush ballad was no longer adequate to mirror the changing outlook of Australian minds. Many writers of the time took to imitating methods established overseas, but O'Dowd struck out independently for a maturer form of utterance than that found in the dominant romanticism of the nineteenth century. "The obstinate independence with which O'Dowd worked out his writing method certainly delayed his development, and made his early writing cruder and flatter than it need have been; on the other hand, it enabled him to develop continuingly. His last work is not a repetition of what he had earlier achieved with the freshness left out, as it is with many poets. It is the final step in the quest for an appropriate style, a quest which started almost from scratch." [18]

Poetry Militant is seen in accurate perspective as a kind of halfway house on O'Dowd's journey in search of development; an important but nevertheless not a final statement of belief. A few years ago, Frederick Macartney set down his memory of the occasion when *Poetry Militant* was first delivered:

On the night of 25th May 1909, when Bernard O'Dowd read his presidential address to the Literature Society of Melbourne in the Masonic Hall, Collins Street, I was a young man enjoying it in a back seat. The president's address was a special annual event, but even the ordinary monthly meetings in a smaller hall were well attended. A speech by O'Dowd always evoked applause, sometimes almost vociferously. His intense fluent earnestness, with the falsetto of his high tones varying his full chanting intonation, was irrestible.[19]

Every person who heard O'Dowd speak testifies to the compelling effect of his mesmeric chant. Katharine Susannah Prichard, who was also in that hall in 1909 and later to become a leading Australian novelist, remembers O'Dowd rising to speak with "his hair flaming to the white-hot intensity of his passion and faith that poetry, and all literary expression, should be inspired by love and service for humanity," and leaving after his address, "exalted and exhilarated." [20] Victor Kennedy and Nettie Palmer, too, speak of his "easy air of authority" in delivering his plea for militant poetry:

In a sense the personality of the speaker was more striking than his argument which was, after all, chiefly an expansion of what Wordsworth, Shelley and Whitman had said—that poets should assimilate the best thought and knowledge of their day and, reverencing their own oracular function, deal with man's fundamental problems in a mood of high seriousness. The personality of the speaker dominated his audience. He was so plainly a poet himself, with his suggestion of smouldering fire, of profound feeling, of psychic power. In its rolling periods, given music and rhythm by the flexible voice, the address was itself a poem.[21]

After it was all over O'Dowd confided to his admiring young friend, Nettie Palmer, that he had been under doctor's orders to restrain himself, "and restraint in a free message is a big handicap . . ." He was also aware of his own shortcomings as a man and as a poet; many of the deepest interests of his fellow Australians he did not share, and in poetry, there was so little to show for his forty-three years of experience "and so much quartz in that little." Yet he knew "that the masses are, unconsciously, becoming emaciated for lack of the poetry which will *never* reach them while the present poets maintain their exclusive rules as to subject and the importance of matter." [22]

CHAPTER TEN

The Intriguing Balance

CRITICS have seen *The Seven Deadly Sins* as O'Dowd's transitional volume; the bony skeleton, it is said, has taken on poetical flesh.[1] The poet himself thought otherwise, and in a letter to Nettie Palmer, apologized for the deep depression that he considered "has left traces in the numerous carelessnesses, weaknesses, and 'unfinish' of what might (and under happier circumstances would) have been strong work."[2] Not a single critic agrees with this view: "The Celtic spirit sent him wandering to the Dominions of the Boundary, where he heard 'the horns of elf land bravely blowing,' and he came back with less fierceness, less desire to bombard the wicked, and an inclination to frivol now and then."[3] "Less fierceness" probably indicates the loosening of the tight quatrains of the first volumes for a freer flowing pentameter and a new lyrical swing.

"With the *Seven Deadly Sins* came the adoption of the sonnet form for a series of duologues between the critic of the seven sins and the sins themselves, who speak up strongly in their own defence. This sonnet series, therefore, is a set of moral debates, conduced with vigour and vision by both parties."[4] Seven sins should normally require no more than seven sonnets, but O'Dowd uses fourteen, and together with a handful of "other sonnets" builds up a book of 56 pages. In original publication there were two pages to a sin with the case for and against on opposite pages. The attack is opened in the second person, while the reply in defense is direct.

"You bade the Morning Star betray the light," begins the accusation against "Pride." It was Pride who lured Napoleon to the Russian snows, caused the flight of Achilles and further back in time, turned idyllic Eden to woe. Pride with the "Pragmatist Pilates of chameleon Truth," still nests in the tree of knowledge. And readily comes the reply;

> Into the ape I breathed, and you were men:
> Never was night I led not to the morn:
> There is no mount you may not climb with me:

> No god you may not challenge, if he dare
> Immure the soul I lit ere he was born![5]

This is straight argument with fair comment on both sides; it is, as Nettie Palmer wrote, a genuine confrontation. But more than this, the significant adoption of an expressive verse-form seemingly brought a change in accent of speech and rhythm.

"Gluttony," who "makes love base, victorious heroes swine, / And tempts man from his heritage divine," points to his active part in the development of civilized life:

> Comfort ye had not found had I not sought:
> Yea, still had champed the grass, herded in dung,
>   And to some apish woman sated flung
> The husk and slavered bone, had I not taught
> The dainty secrets that my nostrils caught
>   From herb and fruit and flower hidden among
>   Your wastes, and sifted with insatiate tongue
> The finer food that builds the finer thought.

"Avarice" churns "the ooze of every deadly sin" and taints every fine ideal, but may also claim on the other hand, to humanize the raw earth, "Pulsing arterial trade from shore to shore." "Envy" is "the quenchless Will that drives the clod, / Through crystal, mould and brute, to man and God!" And so to the final sin, "Sloth," seen with imagination and penetration by the poet as the consistent betrayer of human endeavour:

> And glamoured poet many a look has sent
> Into those eyeballs bear-brown, somnolent,
> Nor dream that devils in each muddy lake
> Were sucking his devotion in to slake
> The furrowed belly of your fanged content!

I. *The Enlivened Stream*

A great deal has been written about O'Dowd's choice of the sonnet as a poetic form and several of his critics imply, if not openly state, that this is a choice suitable to one who is not highly creative. More percipient writers, such as Frederick Macartney, indicate how the sonnet was not limiting to Bernard O'Dowd:

It is a bigger room into which he has moved from a smaller one, and he enjoys striding about vigorously in it. The results are admirable, unless you merely like the thing done with the utter and mostly vacuous smoothness of the same old way. None of O'Dowd's sonnets is of that usual kind, but even by usual standards they need few excuses, the interceptions enlivening the stream.[6]

The late Professor Todd saw him as "a real poet, looking for a subject and for a form—and finding both in some of his sonnets," largely because the sonnet enforced "if not conciseness, at least limitations." " 'Australia' is a rather confused sonnet, but it does have shape; 'The Quail' is a little too much, but it is economical; and some of O'Dowd's other sonnets are as poems, as wholes, the best things he wrote. Some of the eccentricities still remain but the movement is easier, and the poet usually has a subject." [7] These subjects are firmly presented and the ideas unusually interesting; the breadth of his own ethos, and his wide-ranging, questing and energetic mind, is particularly evident in the sonnet sequence. "In one respect," A. A. Phillips found, " ... his intellectuality ran counter to his purpose of making a didactic appeal to the reader's will. He had the scholar's habit of seeking for the question to pose rather than for the answer to be provided. He liked, too, to poise a contradiction in intriguing balance." [8]

II. *The Adamantine Cosmos*

The formal character of O'Dowd's ethics derived from his study of Kant. An outcome of the philosopher's ethical speculations was his denial of virtue in individual perfection; its locus lay rather "in the just relations of men to each other. What is to be fashioned is a republic of wills." One task of moral law was to teach respect of other persons and to treat men as ends and not means. In one of many paraphrases of Kant's doctrines, Bernard O'Dowd asked whether Australia was a democracy. Democracy, he held, was an ideal of life; democracy is more than political theory, government, lawmaking, and maintaining peace and order in a community. It is an ideal of civic conduct, a way of life, a code of the heart. It is a willing obedience as units of the people to the command of that great philosopher, Kant, that we are never to regard any individual, whatever his race, color, caste, sex, riches or poverty as a mere means to an end, but always an end in himself.[9]

The sonnet "To Immanuel Kant" has been overlooked by critics of *The Seven Deadly Sins*. Both in subject matter and placement in that book, it "sums up" (so O'Dowd told me) the preceding poems:

O You, whose bridge invited me to span
  Serene despair enamoured of his slough,
  Ere gentle eyes became a lens to show
The loving Presence, and the perfect plan!
Copernicus, who leaped the sophists' ban
  In Königsberg a hundred years ago,
  And saw the adamantine cosmos flow
In opal streams WITHIN the mind of man!

Where now, abstracted, stellar spires you view,
  Or teach Laplace young nebulae to plant,
Fill Berkeley's void, or Swedenborg pursue,
  Or pick your steps 'mid Hume's agnostic gins,
  Send here equipped like you another Kant
To gloss these Jekylls and their deadly sins! [10]

In his youth O'Dowd serenely accepted a fatalist notion of the universe in which there was no hope of individual salvation; he was, in fact, "enamoured of his slough." "Ere gentle eyes became a lens to show / The loving Presence and the perfect plan!" refers generally to the poet's return to a belief in Christianity, one which he attributed in part to Kant's revelations in philosophy. Besides being the catalyst of O'Dowd's transformation, Kant also harmonized the conflicting views of philosophers Hume and Berkeley. When considered in relation to the second quatrain, the word "lens" carries a greater weight than the mere idea of the human eye as a window of the brain. Copernicus saw harmony in the universal movement of the planets by means of the telescopic lens, and here Kant *is* "Copernicus, who leaped the sophists' ban." Both great men refused to let the conventions of their respective periods cut their theories to suit. Kant himself defined his position by comparisons he made between his discoveries and those of Copernicus.

"Flow" is the operative word in the lines—"And saw the adamantine cosmos flow / In opal streams WITHIN the mind of man!" Kant was the first philosopher to think of studying the nature of human understanding before taking into account its fruits and may be said to have made solidity flow, to have resolved mysteries. His thought, too, flows through the centuries via men such as Carlyle (in *Sartor Resartus*) to O'Dowd, the Australian poet.

When writing *The Critique of Pure Reason,* Immanuel Kant sat at a window where he could stare at the spires of Königsberg, and so the poet sees the "stellar spires" of *The Critique* reaching towards the heavens of thought and to Christ. In "The Sybil of Silence" of *The Silent Land,* O'Dowd asked: "Through her, saw Kant on steeple-top, / Mirage-like, 'The Critique'?" Kant's teachings have both an astronomical and a philosophical aspect. He influenced the ideas of the astronomer Laplace and refuted the views of Berkeley and Hume. "Berkeley's void" is a world of illusion in which matter does not exist, only mind, and "Hume's agnostic gins" is a reference to the theory of crude materialism, of no mind. Swedenborg propounded the theory that both Hume and Berkeley were right and wrong and could not harmonize their views. Wherever you may be, cries O'Dowd, send another like yourself "To gloss these Jekylls and their deadly sins!"

III. *The Lightnings of Song*

Writing to Nettie Palmer at the end of August 1909, the poet confided "[I] am doubtful now whether to put all sonnets in the book. May decide to print a few short lyrics (sparrow ones but mine own!) as well." [11] A month later he had decided to include the sparrow chirps, as he called them, and gave to his public several of his best-known though lighter poems. O'Dowd turns from his restricted quatrains to an unexpected meditation on a cow:

> This is a rune I ravelled in the still,
> Arrogant stare of an Australian cow—
> "These prankt intruders of the hornless brow,
> Puffed up with strange illusions of their skill
> To fence, to milk, to fatten and to kill,
>   Once worshipped me with temple, rite and vow,
>   Crowned me with stars, and bade rapt millions bow
> Before what abject guess they called my will! [12]

Apt phrasing, rich rhythmical expression, insight, scorn and originality, are terms applied to this poem, but behind it is the memory of the poet's accusation in *Poetry Militant:* "Look around you in your country districts, where intellect, lofty emotion, the vigour of youth, the promise of childhood—everything—are being sacrificed daily to the cult of the cow, the usury of the mortgagee, the lure of the bank-balance, the avarice of the eater of acres!"

The loosening of the verse-form is seen in several of these "miscellaneous" verses in *The Seven Deadly Sins*. There is the quiet dignity of the sonnet "In Memory of Victor J. Daley": "More gravely tamarisk will smile this year, / And sadlier lilac breathe her nuptial lays", and the lively jingle of "The Poet":

And why do we fight for our fellows? For Liberty why do we long?
Because with the core of our nerve-cells are woven the lightnings
of song!
For the poet for ages illumined the animal dreams of our sires,
And his Thought-Become Flesh is the matrix of all our unselfish
desires!

The latter, Walter Murdoch tells us in his Introduction to the collected *Poems*, caused O'Dowd misgivings and a letter to a friend who praised it is quoted:

Your kind words about "The Poet" I read with mixed feelings. The thought is all right, but the form in which I put it? . . . It's as subtle a temptation as I've ever got, for, while I think I could reel off that sort of thing by the yard, I have persistently denied myself the pleasure of doing so for years because I thought that the real Muse didn't like it, and that there was altogether too much of it locally. I felt I could trust myself in this instance, because I wanted to say it and to say it simply, and as nearly logically as possible, to an argumentative circle of run-as-you-read readers . . .

O'Dowd was experimenting with a variety of poetic forms during this transition period. Besides sonnets, he wrote such formal verses as the rondeau, the sestina, the ballade, and the chant royal, with originality and technical competence, but not with the idea, as Inglis Moore remarks, of showing "that he could manage the complex verse structure." He was aware, perhaps more than any other Australian poet, of the tendency to in-breeding in verse. "If everybody writes horse-poems in fourteen-syllabled verse," he told the Melbourne University Literary Society, "there's some danger that the Australian epic will be in that verse and mainly about horses." This equally applied to the "sonnet paddock and in the triolet flower-patch." [13]

And consider the manner, the very effective way, in which he used the tradition-shaped great chant royal in "The Bottom Dog Brigade." Instead of an ornate, graceful address to a prince and his courtiers, O'Dowd relates the facts of wage-slavery, indus-trial disease, and all forms of social injustice to show that the only "royal men" are the forward-looking "rankers of the Bottom Dog Brigade." Even the *Envoi* was not addressed to an earthly prince:

O Love-made-man, 'mid modern apathy
Hosts You have fed, released the women we
  Had stoned, consoled the thief, and devils laid,
As when You levied first in Galilee
  The rankers of the Bottom Dog Brigade! [14]

IV. *Right Side Up*

O'Dowd was a poet of serious intent, a "no-nonsense" poet earnestly hammering out his message, but he was not completely humorless as the sonnet "Auster Rampant!" indicates. For a time he assisted Frank Davison, the editor of *Advance Australia*, by "turning the mangle in the 'Answers to Correspondents' column'" of that magazine. He also wrote a number of articles under the nom-de-plume "Ulimaroa," one of which was a light-hearted refutation of Australia's geographical inferiority.[15] Australia, said O'Dowd, suffers the stigma of an inferior physical situation owing to a conspiracy of "conceited map-makers and effete geographers of the Old World." In short, the earth is wrongly represented with its north side up.

Many reasons were urged why south should be up "in the physical sense, as it is in the racial and intellectual sense." There is more land in the northern hemisphere than in the southern, and as land is heavier than water, the heavier half of the globe is also the lower half. Volcanoes are the chimneys of the world and chimneys go out through the roof. As there are no volcanoes at the north pole and at least one at the south pole, the south must be the roof of the world. Peninsulas are the aspirations of continents and all the great ones point to the south. Why do the largest tidal movements begin in the Southern Ocean? The waters disturbed by the moon's attraction begin to roll downhill. The cross is symbolical of the standard of the world and the effort of civilization has always been to keep down the brute within us. Consequently, we find our planet standing with the Southern Cross above her head and the Great Bear (the brute) beneath her feet. It was the ancients who, in a luminous moment, termed the southern regions of the world the antipodes. Literally, antipodes means the opposite to the feet, which is the head.

These few reasons, O'Dowd concluded, "should be sufficient to satisfy any right-thinking person, and especially any really patriotic Australian, that the position assigned to the north in the universe, is nothing more than a myth; born of ignorance, nurtured by conceit, and now subsidised by envy":

> A larger Argo ploughs our clearer blue!
>   Your Zephyr won no such auroral bride
>   As her I woo! The South is whence the tide
> Springs downhill to refresh the North and you!
> To melt your adamantine basements too,
>   When, as your sagas sang, the flaming-eyed
>   Children of Southern Muspel scatter wide
> Your world, your gods, when Ragnarok is due!
>
> Antipodean? Whew! We are the head,
>   The oceanic head, while you, slung low
>   With lands that scrape the floor of heaven, gaze
> Far o'er the Bull your odd Europa wed,
>   Up to the Chambers of the South where glow
>   Our pennant stars, our wider Milky Ways! [16]

V. *Australia, My Rose!*

Beneath the rather awkward unbending, there was still the serious intent. "Australia Mavourneen," for example, seems to indicate the further development of an idea of Australia that reached its full flowering in parts of "The Bush." O'Dowd in an article printed in 1907, indicated how the poem came to be written: "I had been thinking of [a motto for Australia] myself once, and the first sketch was, 'Australia mavourneen, my heather, my rose!' but instead of distilling that into the ineffable two words, redolent of the old and the new, that would have thrilled me into hope, I followed some seductive siren in the phrase into the delicious but insubstantial mazes of several almost erotic anapestic stanzas." [17] Instead of "the ineffable two words," he offers twenty-eight! No more, he says, shall he seek for the English or Persian fairies, no more conjure with the musical phrase to create the magical thing or summon the gods; the poet has seen a vision in the mirror-blue of the Australian sky. The deep love of legend he had, particularly that of Ireland and King Arthur, departs as he views the beauty of his country:

So, pixies and elves who were gracious or strong,
   When England was all to the children she grew,
And kelpies who glamoured the Highlands so long,
   And fairies of Erin, who beckoned us to
The beach of the sea of the soul! Adieu!
For over an Elfland ye knew not there glows
   A dawn that we saw not, revealing to view
Australia mavourneen, my heather, my rose!

CHAPTER ELEVEN

Sybil and Siren

SHORTLY after *The Bush* appeared in book form, the *Bulletin* described it as a complete prospectus for the importation, for poetic purposes, of a consignment of seasoned and well-authenticated gods. Then the article went on in the same manner:

Here's a bare patch of land, eminently suitable for gods, that has been left uncultivated since the beginning of time. The Bush must be populated with imported mythological beings; our nation is ready to welcome them; and there seems no reasonable doubt but that the gods of antiquity can be successfully acclimatized, while in due time there is every possibility that, in the favourable environment of Australia, they will produce new gods, true Australian gods, who will no longer speak of Greece and Norway as "Home." [1]

In the course of this burlesque, the same writer speaks of the "commonplace catalogue of contemporary names in order to emphasize the poet's view that Romance is now." A careful reading of the poem shows this statement to be quite false; first, it indicates a deliberate misunderstanding of the purpose of that "catalogue," and second, to single out for severe handling a mere sixty lines of a total 670 is, to say the least, wilful criticism. Inglis Moore, for example, finds the first portion of the poem "long drawn out and treated with a detail and in a manner that produces. . . . poetic curiosities." O'Dowd simply regarded these passages as a suitable extravagance and did not expect his obviously far-fetched parallels to be taken in deadly earnest.[3] The truth of the matter is that many have never bothered to understand the purpose of this section of *The Bush* and have been clumsy and impercipient in ignoring both the humor of the lines and their action in qualifying the later, and major, portion of the poem.

I. *Communion to Thanksgiving*

There is a freer use of verse structure in *The Bush*, but this change had, in the wide sense, been taking place for some years.

O'Dowd told me of many influences that helped in causing the
change, mentioning in particular remarks such as those of Mr.
Justice Higgins, who, "speaking like a good equity lawyer," suggested "the ship is a bit too light for the cargo." The reason concerning the reader must be sought in the poem itself, and is
simply its appropriateness. The individual stanzas reflect the
movement of the theme throughout the long poem; "it sways and
returns on its tenacious central trunk," said Frederick Macartney.[4] This same writer speaks of the "mystic aroma" and "the
yearning doubt" of The Bush, which are significant phrases with
an added significance when one realizes that The Bush approx-
imates the Mass of Catholic worship and covers all the major
divisions from the offering of adoration to atonement and im-
petration. Like the Mass, it begins with a statement of belief
and preparatory prayers and ends with the communion and the
hymn of thanksgiving.

Victor Kennedy and Nettie Palmer point to the clear and remarkable unity of the poem:

This unity showed, first, on the surface, in its definite and exceptional
form. Here was a long poem of sixty-seven ten-lined pentameter stanzas. Each stanza contained, first, a quatrain rhymed alternately; then,
like a keystone to an arch, a taut rhymed couplet; last, another quatrain with alternate rhymes but this time the first and third lines
rhyming always with a double ending.[5]

There is also a deeper uniformity of matter and of argument.
The poem opens with a youthful impression of the appearance
of trees as beings, or more particularly, as persons at prayer.
This idea is also present in the third main section when the
bush is seen as a "great / Pillared cathedral tremulously green"
(line 252). In the haze "we seem to see / Tangible Presences
of Deathless Things":

> Across each terraced aeon Time hath sowed
>   With green tautology of vanished years,
> Gaping aghast or webbed with shining lode,
>   Achilles' anger's earthquake-rift appears.
>   (lines 21-24)

This accords with the poet's stated view of modern civilization
resting on classical literature as "the common language of humanity," and without which poets "will degenerate into rhapso-

dists of an obscure dialect without traditions and without universality...." [6]

II. *Hellas of the Present*

To an insensitive observer the bush may suggest only the seclusion of desolation, but the poet feels it moulding and influencing our lives, and the certainty that it holds both "strange shapes of reproof and portent and omen," and all the "potentialities of future Australian Romance":[7]

> Yea, Mother Bush, in your deep dreams abide
> Cupids alert for man and maid unborn,
> Apprentice Pucks amid your saplings hide,
> And wistful gorges wait a Roland horn:
> Wallet of Sigurd shall this swag replace,
> And centaurs curvet where those brumbies race.
> That drover's tale of love shall greaten duly
> Through magic prisms of a myriad years,
> Till burns Isolde to Tristram's fervour newly,
> Or Launcelot to golden Guinevere's.
>
> (lines 31-40)

But Troy "hath ever been"; in other times, other names, yet always associated with movement and human striving. Half-seriously O'Dowd once suggested "there is no reason why [Australia] should not be the Hellas of the present. Our climate is that of Greece; our outdoor life, our love of athletics, our well-diffused educational opportunities, our keenness in political matters, are all those of the Greeks..." [8] To emphasize his idea, the poet makes use of a cyclic or "terraced" time, in which history is the "tautology of vanished years." A little later he has reinforced this notion sufficiently to support the statement that all change will appear to future Australians as one antiquity, and "The humdrum lives that now we tire of, then / Romance shall be, and we heroic men / Treading the vestibule of Golden Ages..."

It was this aspect of *The Bush* that led Professor Chisholm to name the poem a landmark at "the beginning of a new poetic vision of Australia."

... it lifts us out of the immediate and thus makes up for our (comparative) lack of history. It brings out the fact that Australian culture is rooted in a very ancient past, and moving on towards a very long future, thus transcending the brief awkwardness of colonialism, and putting itself into the long perspective of anthropological time. And therein, precisely, lies the real greatness of *The Bush*, which is a mixture of naive nostalgias and deep-reaching visions.[9]

It was Professor Chisholm, too, who enlarged upon O'Dowd's use of Eternal Recurrence as a fundamental part of the philosophical structure of *The Bush*: "The main argument of the poem is, in fact, a special statement of this doctrine. Just as the Greek heroic age had provided the raw material of the later Hellenic myths and romances, so too, according to Mr. O'Dowd, the things we are doing today, the things that the pioneers did yesterday, are the material out of which the future Romance of Australia will be woven." [10] For the moment, however, he is content with the omens and auguries of Homer's *Iliad*.

III. *The Towers of Phoebus*

While settlers cleared the mountainous country where Troy was to be built, Homer told the story of its future greatness; so the poet sings of the Australia to be while nation-building is in progress. Similarly, Minoan art, seen as a Garden of Eden or aboriginal Alcheringa (in the Dream Time), produced a Briseis (prize of Achilles) long before Homer's advent. Again, the Sumerians, predecessors of the Babylonians, had their god of poetry who "song built" a legend of Chaldea's future greatness. O'Dowd's practice in *The Bush* was not, as Macartney said, to pile image on image, but to present an idea or a situation and then set off a succession of associated images that not only charges the narrative with a necessary amount of density and gives the effect of a litany, but also moves it forward. He introduces the "willowed water" of Babylon (Psalm 137:1-4) for this purpose, and the reference has just the right touch for a passage dealing with Homeric conquest. The name Phoebus carries more meaning than just a vague indication of a Greek god, since this is another title for Apollo, god of Troy, and who, especially in Homer, is a god of prophecy. In addition, he brought back sunshine and light in the Spring. He was also the founder of States and a leader of colonies, and so his oracle may be said to sanction the work of colonists in new settlements.

The line "The towers that Phoebus builds can never fall," may refer to his building of the walls of Troy or to the enduring qualities of his work as a god of art and culture; again, in conjunction with the next line in the stanza, it might be read as having sexual connotations. "The sons of God, beholding Leda's daughter, / Bartered eternal thrones for love of her," can be treated in the same manner; the sons of God gave up the love of God for human beauty as represented by Helen of Troy. The Biblical reference is easily discernible: "That the sons of God saw the daughters of men that they were fair; and they took them wives of all which they chose" (Genesis 6:2).

Nevertheless, the poet sees this love as an ideal kind that can "never pall," and seen in this way, must be protected by the goddess Aphrodite. His example is in keeping with the previous stanzas and drawn from the *Iliad*. In that epic, Paris, son of King Priam of Troy, ran away with Helen of Argos and when wounded in battle by Diomedes was carried off by Aphrodite. If the mystery of the bush encourages O'Dowd to conjure up an Homeric dream of love and war, can he avoid the frightening omen of the death and mutilation of the Trojan hero Hector? Although he had a presentiment of the fall of his country, it will be remembered that Hector continued his resistance in preference to death, slavery, or disgrace.

IV. *Myriad Magic Prisms*

Lines thirty to sixty sum up the vision of the trees; the poet moves down time as signified by great romances of the past to the raw material of romances to be:

> That drover's tale of love shall greaten duly
> Through magic prisms of a myriad years,
> Till burns Isolde to Tristram's fervour newly,
> Or Launcelot to golden Guinevere's.

In stanza five O'Dowd uses a kind of "catalogue" passage to portray lusty growth, just as Walt Whitman used heterogeneity to celebrate formlessness. The technique in comparable passages implies the teeming variety of a new country:

> The miner cradling washdirt by the creek,
> Or pulled through darkness dripping to the plat:
> The navvy boring tunnels through the peak:
> The farmer grubbing box-trees on the flat:
> The hawker camping by the roadside spring:
> The hodman on the giddy scaffolding:

Moths that around the fashion windows flutter:
The racecourse spider and the betting fly:
The children romping by the city gutter,
While baby crows to every passer-by.

(lines 41-50)

From "these rough blocks," he says, future legends will be chiselled; "Romance shall be," not as the *Bulletin* reviewer wrote, "Romance is now."

As the opening section of *The Bush* finishes, "the gospel of the day" begins. By way of illustration, O'Dowd instances how our cultural past and our present may appear to merge at a point in time future. These seven stanzas are those so adversely mentioned by critics, who commonly brush this portion aside as an elaborate conceit. Originally limited to the ten lines of stanza seven, the writer decided to follow the example of Homer in the catalogue of ships and similar methods used by Whitman, and give Australian writers, artists, and scholars a little advertisement. Besides the clever compressed references to his contemporaries, the stanzas deserve their place as a means of consolidating the leading ideas of the preceding section. Also, they introduce a slightly more intimate note and presage the long personal fourth section of the poem.

While contact is maintained with what has gone before, O'Dowd introduces a major figure of what is to follow; the Sappho mentioned is not merely the leader of the Aeolian school of Greek poetry, but also Marie Pitt, to whom he gave the same name: "Out of some singing woman's heart-break plea / Australia's dawn shall flush with Sappho's rose."

Shirlow, in times to come, will be confused with Raphael's etcher, Mantegna, and Victor Daley's verse celebrations of wine with the nectar of the gods. Louis Esson's plays will appear as fragments of prehistoric drama, and the sculpture of Web Gilbert as monuments of religious worship. Hugh McCrae will be regarded as the leader of his own creations in his book *Satyrs and Sunlight,* while Frank Williamson's poem "The Magpie's Song" is equated with the pipes of Pan, and Henry Kendall's mourning for his daughter Araluen is as memorable as any Irish keening. The parson-poet, Hebblethwaite, is seen as a "Tasmanian Wordsworth" riding about his parish. (The poem mentioned is "Perdita," which was based on Shakespeare's *The Winter's Tale*).

New Zealand poetess Jessie Mackay "sees the elves deploy in kern and gallowglass" near Mount Cook. The scholar is assumed to be the author of works he has translated. So too does mathematics Professor Pirani merge with the philosopher Pythagoras. In classical mythology, Marsyas was skinned by Apollo for criticizing him, but here is the victim of Rhadamanthine (Judge of Hell) "Stephens' steady blade." A. G. Stephens, of course, was the notable Australian literary critic and editor. Again, Frank Morton and Benvenuto Cellini are associated by a claim to have seen or by having written a story about a salamander. Spencer, besides being a student of aboriginal lore, was a member of the Horn expedition to Central Australia. Edwin Brady, a sea-balladist, is seen pushing his Viking ships ("Long Snakes") through southern waters. Dowell O'Reilly had always championed Sydney against the supposed dullness of O'Dowd's home-city Melbourne, and so the poet retaliates by bringing Sydney into conjunction with Sybaris—a byword in love of luxury and pleasure in the ancient world. Professor Walter Murdoch as essayist and literary critic is confused with Longinus, author of a book on the Sublime and the Beautiful and an adviser to Zenobia, queen of Palmyra. Judge Way of South Australia and a translator of Homer into galloping verse, translates his author into his original tongue. The historical character of Cromwell's time shares leadership with Vern, believed by O'Dowd to be "the true hero of Eureka," and nineteenth century radicals Ben Tillett and Tom Mann cannot be distinguished from Wat Tyler and Jack Cade. In the same manner Dowie, once a Collingwood churchman who later founded a religious sect in America, becomes mixed with Cagliostro.

V. *Guides to the Grail*

Progressing to questions of reform, O'Dowd begins with the legend of Tarpeia who was tempted by the golden Sabine bracelets and collars to open the fortress' gates, and of Cataline, the poverty-stricken but unscrupulous Roman politician. The Roman reformers have the facial characteristics of Longmore, a Victorian land-reformer and sometime Minister for Lands. "The wealthy lower orders" was an expression applied to the opponents of social betterment by Higginbotham and Don, according to the poet "the first real Labor member" of parliament, commonly used a saying about what would happen when the stockwhip cracks.

Parliamentarians are notorious for betraying election promises, but when accorded royal notice become "Cleons in Windsor

dress at Syracuse"; demagogues akin to Cleon who went to
Syracuse and opposed peace during the Peloponnesian war.
"Rose Scott refutes dogmatic Cyril gaily, / Hypatia turns the
anti-suffrage flank." Cyril of Alexandria tried to remove Hypatia
for seeking rights for women, but is refuted by the existence of
a Sydney suffragette named Rose Scott.

There is a danger in dismissing these sixty lines merely as an
elaborate conceit. Read in their context they fill the mind as
ample illustration of "southern glows." The ancients with whom
they are brought into conjunction also represent O'Dowd's interests in art and politics and are not just a "consignment" of
miscellaneous gods of antiquity. Further, the persons mentioned
assist with a suggestion of a more complex attitude and so adds
to the effective structure of the poem which, regarded in the
light of action, seeks a unity of faith by dramatic resolution.
While seemingly in conflict among themselves, all the examples
do point to some ideal of creation, of love, or of thought.

The Bush in many of its basic ideas, like so much of O'Dowd's
work, derives from even earlier attempts at the same theme, in
this instance from "Austrelaine: The Fairy of the Gully," which
was written for an entertainment at the Australian Church. This
poem opens with verses very close to the ideas expressed in
The Bush:

> From ancient causeways stretch our modern roads,
>   From ancient error modern science flowers,
> Old legal founts supply our modern codes;
> Old temples' stones we've reared "august abodes,"
>   Where love, with sacred light, the modern dowers.
>
> And myths antique have functions still where we
>   May teem a virgin soil with fruit and grain;
> So, moulded to a form we fain would see,
> Where ambient air is "catholic and free,"
>   Springs on our stage the fairy, Austrelaine.

And even closer comes the following verse:

> Where wild swans seek the freshening storm afar,
>   Or jackass laughs alike in joy or woe,
> Where curlew's Banshee shrieks the midnight mar,
>   Or lyre-birds dance amid the bush bazaar,
>   With all the notes its myriad linguists know.

These five lines make up the "observations" in stanza thirteen of *The Bush*. The extinction of the wild turkey once so plentiful about Beaufort parallels the certain failure of the individual visions sketched in the previous section of the poem; like the "regal bustard" they will be remembered only to the extent they are absorbed in legend.

The lyre-bird, jackass, and curlew are all associated with the worship of Dionysus the tree spirit. As he was a god worshipped with loud cries, the "feathered Pan" makes the Bacchanalian cry, "Evoe." The curlews, whom the youthful poet had thought of as banshees, are here followers of Bacchus. Beyond these obvious references it should be noted that Dionysus was also the possessor of oracular powers second only to Apollo, and in primitive art was represented as a figure partly tree and partly man. In another legend, he is said to have descended to the underworld and then returned with his mother, this being regarded as symbolizing future life and a triumph over death. It is this myth that O'Dowd uses in the later sections of the poem when he draws upon his personal experiences of youthful ideals and mature love.

While apparently dealing with bush birds in stanza thirteen he throws up further allusions to Troy as a continuation of the opening section. When Sarpedon was killed at the siege of Troy, swans bore him away to the west, and Memnon, son of the Dawn and native of the land of the sun in the extreme south of the world, in post-Homeric legend is an Egyptian who was also killed at Troy.

VI. *Sadness Behind Creation*

The fairy of the gully "forms our units' chaos into men," but the poet asks whether the theory that with each succeeding generation the new inhabitants tend to approximate the aboriginals is true—the American to the Red Indian, the Australian to the blackfellow. This idea might be considered an augury of future mingling and sympathy between man and nature. Not all heed the signs; even those who realize the power of environment forget in times of happiness and well-being the sadness behind creation when "Your harps, unblurred by glozing strings, intone / The dirges that behind Creation moan."

Two common views of the relationship between the inhabitants of a country and their environment are expressed. The first is of a land exploited by the "avaricious plough," where the wild

spread of the bush and the vast growth of trees is replaced by
tame orchards, shrubbery, and ordered plantations more suited
to older settlements. Secondly, there is the idea that the bush
has a sinister aspect until the settlers of the land endow it with
the harmony of human living. Lines 67-8 refer to Milton's mourning for *Lycidas:*

> But O the heavy change, now thou art gone,
> Thee Shepherd, thee the Woods, and desert Caves,
> With wilde Thyme and the gadding Vine o'er grown,
> And all their echoes mourn.

This is the fruit of no-faith, but the door to heaven is readily
opened: "Ask, and it shall be given you; seek, and ye shall find;
knock, and it shall be opened unto you: For every one that
asketh receiveth; and he that seeketh findeth; and to him that
knocketh it shall be opened." [11]

O'Dowd's echo of the Sermon on the Mount is a natural balance to the implied results of misbelief and lack of harmony;
he sets forth God's mercy and vengeance in the manner of Moses,
pointing to faith as the rock of salvation: "... and he made him
to suck honey out of the rock, and oil out of the flinty rock." [12]
But when men worship strange gods, "new gods that came newly
up," and cease to "consider their latter end" they must suffer
and expiate their sin. Men, as yet, have only accepted the
"poignant tones and sombre strength" of the bush, without hear-
ing the infinite variety of its many voices. Their misguided way
of living, their failure to realize the land serves no purpose but
its own, is not slave but free, is evidenced in the remains of
their attempts at exploitation; polluted creeks and upturned earth
at Beaufort and paddocks at Broadmeadows laden with night-
soil are typical. Not all, however, have sought to master the bush;
to others she is the mother church to be treated with respect and
piety.

Stanza twenty-five marks a major change in *The Bush:* what
has been an undertone in the earlier verses rises to importance:

> As many, Mother, are your moods and forms
>   As all the sons who love you. Here, you mow
> Careering grounds for every brood of storms
>   The wild sea-mares to desert stallions throw;
> Anon, up through a sea of sand you glance
>   With green ephemeral exuberance,

And then quick seeds dive deep to years of slumber
From hot-hoofed drought's precipitate return:
There, league on league, the snow's cold fingers number
The shrinking nerves of supple-jack and fern.

The bush has as many aspects as the men and women who
know her. She is the virgin solitude "where the gods we make
by our virtues and our powers shall abide and cherish us forever";[13] she is the prophetess whose ambiguous message must be
spelt out from the arrangement of her leaves; she is the soil
which will bear food to nourish us, and the "virgin womb unsoiled by ancient fear" that will, in time, bear a "Great Australia":

We love our brothers, and to heal their woe
Pluck simples from the known old gardens still:
We love our kindred over seas, and grow
Their symbols tenderly o'er plain and hill:
We feel their blood rebounding in our hearts,
And speak as they would speak our daily parts:
But under all we know, we know that only
A virgin womb unsoiled by ancient fear
Can Saviours bear. So, we, your Brahmins, lonely,
Deaf to the barren tumult, wait your Year.
(lines 321-330)

VII. *Sybil and Siren*

The Bush progresses from descriptions of the wonder and
strangeness of her charms and lyrical exultation of her mysteries to a series of highly subjective revelations of what the
bush had meant to O'Dowd personally:

Throughout the centre of the poem there is a wavering between the
conception of the Bush as a living force that will shape its inhabitants with its spirit, steeping their learning in its own lore, moulding
them ideals for attainment, and of a virgin womb to bear Saviours,
an empty scroll on which the future can be written. There is no war-
fare between the two conceptions. *The Bush* is not a rational argument but a symphony in which now one aspect is emphasised, now
another. The changes in its feeling give it balance and movement:
the varying nature of its images give it density and strength.[14]

And so she changes; mother and lover, "Sybil and Siren, with
alternate breaths," both good and evil:

Yea, you are all that we may be, and yet
    In us is all you are to be for aye!
The Giver of the gifts that we shall get?
    An empty womb that waits the wedding day?
This drifting sense by age-long habit buoyed
Plays round the thought that knows all nature void!
And so, my song alternate would believe her
    Idiot Bush and daughter of the Sun,
A worthless gift apart from the receiver,
    An empty womb, but in a Deathless One.
                              (lines 601-610)

Australia is not yet, but the Bush is full of omens and auguries
of Her. Yet Nature is at best only a "willing plasm," "matrix
inert," and the future will be determined chiefly by the human
will, by the kind of ideals held by men:

Yet she shall be as we, the Potter, mould:
    Altar or tomb, as we aspire, despair:
What wine we bring shall she, the chalice, hold:
    What word we write shall she, the script, declare:
Bandage our eyes, she shall be Memphis, Spain:
Barter our souls, she shall be Tyre again:
And if we pour on her the red oblation
    All o'er the world shall Asshur's buzzards throng:
Love-lit, her Chaos shall become Creation:
    And dewed with dream, her silence flower in song.

CHAPTER TWELVE

For Love Alone

SEVEN years after publication of *The Bush*, Bernard O'Dowd's last major work appeared. *Alma Venus!* may have been his final statement in any case, since he had treated in some form or another the important themes, but its hostile reception by a dozen or so reviewers indicated to him how much out of fashion his poetry was. Apart from the collected editions of his verse, nothing further appeared in book form, and printings in magazines and newspapers were very occasional indeed.

The basic idea behind *Alma Venus!* made many appearances in O'Dowd's poetry. "Venus Genetrix" in *Dominions of the Boundary* claims for herself the source of life:

> Wherever beats the pulse of life
> In rushing Cosmos' plan,
> I am the mother and the wife
> Of every god and man . . .

"Lust" in *The Seven Deadly Sins* is the same person as Venus:

> Yes, when upon my noonday shrine ye can
> Your sweet oblations frank and faithful burn,
> The veil that darkens God shall lift from man,
> Sin shall depart, the Golden Age return.

In *Alma Venus!* the same conception has been widened and deepened in a true fusion of thought, feeling and imagination:

> Love we or dread, we may not all ignore
> The single beacon on the circling shore
> Where being laps upon the caverned steep
> Wherefrom we drifted and whereto we creep.

What is Life? O'Dowd could not find a satisfactory answer when, as a young man, he addressed the Melbourne Lyceum on "Life and its Duties." "When the earth was young and our race

was in babyhood," he said, "savage men in rudely-shaped boats
on silent lakes asked this same question as they carried their
dead comrade to his tomb in the deep. And in our day the same
question is asked by our wisest men, and great as is the differ-
ence between the savage and the philosopher, they have both
been compelled to admit that they could not answer it." Sixty
years later, while still not certain, he did feel he had discovered
one clue to the riddle of human living.

Alma Venus! is organized around thoughts about the heavenly
Uranian Venus and Venus Pandemos, the Venus of this world.
Both, the poet suggests, are valid objects of reverence and can-
not properly be separated:

> Trembling Creation's omnipresent sun,
> Immanent Harmonist, whose rhythms run
> Alike where midge pursues his swift romance,
> Or grave stars cluster for their midnight dance!

This fundamental conception of O'Dowd's has been generally
considered trite, even banal; "the amazing thing about *Alma
Venus!*," complained David McKee Wright, "is how slight a
thought can be padded out to such an inordinate length without
any resort to imagination or one clear word-picture of anything." [1] The same writer makes a great deal of what he terms
O'Dowd's dictionary method of singing: "Having mentioned
Venus he immediately reels off everything that has the least con-
nection with her or with the idea her deity stands for. This fills
space rapidly and makes thought quite unnecessary: also it
makes reading somewhat difficult."

An anonymous reviewer (undoubtedly A. G. Stephens) in the
Bookfellow (December, 1921) summed up *Alma Venus!* as a
"catalogue of historical references to sex, with a commentary
containing some good Hudibrastic lines" but "too much futile
word spinning." More strange was the coldness of Walter Murdoch, who was later to write a glowing introduction to the collected *Poems*. With schoolmasterly severity he denounced *Alma
Venus!* as simply "one more contribution to chaos": "He has
given us a powerful and poetic statement of the mysteriousness
of sex, and if he chooses to use the mark of interrogation as a
means presenting the mystery, why should he not? My reply is
that *Alma Venus!* is not a powerful and poetic statement of anything at all."

I. *The Riddle of the Universe*

Man's place in the universe presents itself in many questions which are indifferently answered with creeds and aphorisms that lightly side-step the real issues. In this long poem, O'Dowd does not dodge issues, but neither does he answer; he illuminated an idea, and wrote a hymn of adoration rather than a precise treatise. His fundamental notion appears to be, as has been stated above, the identity of the "Venus force" with God, or primal creative force. The poem is not a song of sex, mysterious or otherwise; the dominant note is one of glorification of the deity responsible for the Creation and of its identity with the lesser "Venus force" which is the obvious and most familiar example of its existence. O'Dowd offers no solution to the sex problem, and oddly enough, as A. D. Ellis remarked, the poem is also deficient in that it gives no solution to the Far Eastern problem, the economic problem, or even the domestic servant problem! With fine fire and essential dignity he does proclaim the universal sway of the "Venus force" and surveys the whole of creation for signs of her.

Following his opening section, O'Dowd launches into the drama of fertility with Venus Pandemos hovering as a presence over the half-forgotten rites celebrated in Europe—and Australia:

> That fertile gods, unshackled by their play,
> From winter death will duly be reborn
> And with their foison fill the ears of corn:
> Or where, horizonward, Australian sand
> Billows monotonous, behold Your band
> Of leaf-clad lubras, swaying to the hum
> Of droning wizard and barbaric drum,
> In strange Unthippa dance to conjure there,
> With warm wild posturing and coy despair,
> Some dream-time god of golden ages dim,
> That with the drama of their love for him
> The waste in sympathy will fertile grow,
> Emu be plentiful, the dry creeks flow,
> And all the wild be rich with nut and plant,
> Witchetty grub and root and honey-ant.

This conception has been reduced by critics to the simple statement: lust rules humanity. "This note in nature is surely obvious enough without emphatic statement," complained David McKee

Wright, "but the claim that it is the keynote of everything which humanity has found worth while and of all that man has done through the ages is, to say the least of it, an extraordinary theme for a didactic poem." [2] Another writer could find "no all-pervading idea" in *Alma Venus!* to attack; it was merely a mass of conundrums: "there is some sort of philosophic idea about love. There is some struggling revelation that would bring light on dark parts of human experience were it not that the secret is unrevealed, and the poet's profound and intense fervor swells into what is very like foaming incoherence." [3]

Apparently these two and many others, felt that O'Dowd was serving up a reheated dish from his poetic kitchen. He had previously written of "Cupid" as an amoral life-force and "Juno" as a careful goddess who had evolved codes of morality for the protection of the family from the universal spawning impulse. And in *Poetry Militant* he had called for poets to explore with delicate lancets the great mystery: "The Song of Sex has got to be sung, reverently sung, for the problems of sex, being part of the mystery of creation, are perhaps the most interesting of all to every truly normal individual. . . ." The critics looked no further than the lines:

> Austere Mohammed meets at Heaven's door
> Fond phantoms of his desert dreams of yore:
> The shrine, the song, the picture and the bust
> Are diamond doubles of the charcoal, lust.

II. *The Simplicity of Sincerity*

O'Dowd turns to the more ideal aspects of Venus after making his revelation and in a spontaneous and beautiful lyric vibrating with an inner intensity he hymns the divinity as:

> Door of our existence, beacon of our haze,
>   Horn of beatitude, clue to the maze,
> Pole for the magnet, chalice of the Quest,
>   Ark of the wilderness, star of the West,
> Moon of our dream-tide's pallid solitudes,
>   Builder of homes and harmonist of feuds,
> Crowned with the stars and throned upon the night,
> Mother of dolour dearer than delight,
>   Storm in the lily's virginal repose,
>   Flame of the amethyst, breath of the rose,
> First foam and fairest from the far Deep flung,
>   Ancient of Days, perpetually young!

The subtle change in meter and rhythm in this section of the poem is very effective and caused T. Inglis Moore to exclaim over the bold maintenance of the heroic couplet, "line after line, upon an emphatic basis of triumphant dactyls."

However, the movement of *Alma Venus!* is not simply one of straight line progression from primitive darkness to celestial light; quite dramatically and positively O'Dowd speaks of the community of origin of good and evil, but sees no sharp conflict or triumph, one over the other. They are aspects of one figure. The living wheel we call creation, one image says, has Venus Pandemos at the hub while the fires of Venus Immaculate glow from the circumference. Trees of knowledge set in Nile mud by "incestuous Isis" sometimes still bear poisonous fruit:

> Mandrakes beneath Your altar moaning grow,
> And raven ribbons blemish Iris' bow:
> There is a wail inwoven with Your song,
> Shadowy tigers draw Your car along
> Where doves are wont to be—

There are perversions of certain elements of the "Venus force" in creative art that must be absorbed:

> Misshapen Muses, interloping, smear
> The painter's vision with salacious leer,
> With tints obscene the sculptured form pollute,
> To a lewd delirium the dance transmute,
> Contort to brothel taste Your breast and hips,
> With bawdy poison redden Music's lips,
> And tamper with the pure and sparkling flow
> Of Song—

Mankind does not simply reproduce, live, and die; there is some cause for our persistent faith in immortality:

> There is something in us will elude
> The withering fingers of vicissitude,
> And man's ripe earth by a guttering sun betrayed
> Will not in cold and useless ruin fade.

What? Who can answer? Will the "dazzling veil" we call reality be drawn aside to reveal the meaning of life; will good and evil "kiss and understand"; will "God walk with Satan hand in hand?"

What blazing Word dissolves the mystery?
What feet anointed walk our turbid sea?
What moley in the moaning thicket grows?
What prism can the gloom divide or throws
One gleam of light from one unswerving star
Upon the area where, unasked, we are
Merely the drops of unregarded blood
Flecked from unending frays of doltish mud
And idiot lightning purposelessly breeding
Mimes for the masques of Entities unheeding—
Unresting swingers of dark pendulums,
Afreets of those relentless vacumms
Ambushed within the core of all things dense,
Who shall with lingering omnipotence
Suck every mote and orb that sail the Deep
Into the harbour of a point to sleep. . . .

III. *The Beating Heart*

Alma Venus! concludes in the manner we have been led to
anticipate. The eternal and insoluble problems of the Creation
and of its ultimate purpose have baffled all inquiries but we
recognize "One signal flashing from the Outer Vast"—"beget or
bear!" The earliest manuscript dated 19 May 1914, ended—

The pregnant Night, the brooding Day are soundless
The awful sea of silence stretches boundless

But dim the beating heart amid its sighing
Is "Alma Venus! Alma Venus!" crying
And from the sibyl's cavern no leaves fly
But one enscrolled "Increase and multiply."

Seven years later, in rewriting and completing the poem, O'Dowd
had difficulty in expressing his conclusion:

While on two sibyl leaves by a whirlwind strange
Blown to our shore across the Gulf of Change
Are written clear on one in ochre
"Increase and multiply" and on [the other]
Beneath the nimbus of a brooding dove
In gold imperishable "God is Love."

Following many attempts he achieved the lines as printed:

But dim the beating heart amid its sobs
With "Alma Venus!" "Alma Venus!" throbs;

> While on two sibyl leaves, by a world-wind strange
> Blown to our shore across the gulf of Change,
> "Increase and multiply" on one is scrolled
> In ochre crude, on one, in glowing gold
> Around the pearly nimbus of a dove,
> The script imperishable—"God is Love."

O'Dowd's productions were invariably a matter of some public interest, but the reception given to *Alma Venus!* was disconcerting to the poet who spoke of the "one-eyed, paltry and theological criticisms," and "theological banalities and very unkind personalities" he had thrown at him by reviewers.[4] He did not attempt to answer these publicly, but in a letter to Nettie Palmer in March 1922 he denied that his poem was didactic in any sense; it was a garland for the head:

Even in a poem which sets out to be a "coronal-laying" job (and is therefore *not* didactic) isn't the suggestion that Venus is the Demiurge (at least) and that Darwin's theory or hypothesis of "sexual selection" adds an element of certainty to Lucretius and the Cabalists something more than "tentative"? Is the basing of all religions on the creative instincts merely "tentative"? May it be possible that a modern poem may by indirection and questions, assert the Advent of an old Deity anew? Nay, may not new Korans of the Oneness of Deity take the form of a poem asking questions to which there are in all theology, no answers but uncomfortable ones?

Why not "say straight out that reproduction is the only evidence of purpose of God, or of anything in the material universe?" O'Dowd asked.

Almost nine years prior to his letter to Nettie Palmer, O'Dowd had written to Frederick T. Macartney an even more pointed note that does much to light the intellectual background of *Alma Venus!*:

I am pretty sure that when all the religions of the world have played their part and faded, the great Mystery that is yet near to us all will reassert itself as a God again, and the worship of Venus, Aphrodite, or what you like to call Her/Him/It, will again, purified by age-long silences and frosts and snows, be the world-wide religion of the whole race. It is the one thing, for *certain* we are here for, and the symbol of How Much behind what we see or ever shall see of the Things Beyond.[5]

IV. *Cisterns of the Flesh*

"What is it all about?" is the title to a page of manuscript
found in a trunk full of literary and personal effects after
O'Dowd's death. The prose glose is undated and punctuation
has been added:

> What is it all about? To make men trustful of the ultimate rightness
> of it all.
> You mean really what is it all as concerned with you and those
> you are concerned with. Who can be real here where all is unreal,
> even man's mind? For where are the minds of all those who were
> here when nation's unknown were conquered by nations also engulfed
> in mysterious silences? Out of all springs nothing, as out of nothing
> sprang all. You are only you because no one loved no one. No one
> knows when or where, and who whom you know came otherwise?
> Parents know not their children, for continuity is not through a pipe
> of flesh but through a pipe of thinking, and who remembers what his
> and her thoughts were when junction of their cells took place, per-
> haps hours after their flesh fused? Who can be born of man when
> infinite thoughts go to his making? And who can be born of woman
> when myriad men were dimly united with myriad women, each con-
> tributing to the pattern?

All this, of course, does not explain or substitute for the poem
itself; no commentary or paraphrase can ever do so.

Alma Venus! was O'Dowd's only considerable poem to follow
The Bush, and although he was occasionally in print as a poet
after 1922 (some of the results appear in the collected *Poems*,
pp. 239-64), he was essentially retired as a writer. Doubtless
this was partly due to the violent attacks made upon *Alma
Venus!*, but more so to the fact that he had said in verse all that
he wished to say. Also, as Kennedy and Palmer indicate, his
mood and technique were out of tune with the growing generation of readers and critics. "The 'modern' movement that influenced most poets writing in the twenties was," they wrote, "in
part, a reaction against traditional forms: it aimed at the cultiva-
tion of a verse that was free, that discarded rhyme and hypnotic
rhythms, that shunted words and attitudes hitherto regarded as
poetic. It disliked the sonorous and the rhetorical and clung as
closely as possible to the cadences of colloquial speech." [6]

Yet *Alma Venus!*, written in a couplet form of considerable
grace, represented O'Dowd's "prosodic emancipation" and a
progression in form and ideas, but lacked the smooth flow and

easy confidence of *The Bush*. Many lines are too tight and harsh
with crowded syllables, the piling up of instances and epithets
often mechanical, but nevertheless the poem is rich in striking
images freshly minted from the natural world and history, such
as: "Celibate piety with thumb uncouth / Plastered a fig-leaf over
Plato's truth" and powerful metaphorical epigrams as "The
tower impregnable that masters Fate / Is not Caesar but the
celibate." In fact, O'Dowd's wealth, abundance, and power of
phrase and comparison are perhaps his most remarkable traits
and are exceptional in Australian poetry.

There is an unfortunate rhetorical emphasis in a few passages,
particularly the section beginning "When Love was driven from
the world by stark / And sexless mattoids of the Ages Dark," but
most of the poem does not attempt indoctrination. Again, the
charge of conscious erudition is commonly levelled against
O'Dowd in *Alma Venus!;* certainly there are many historical and
other allusions in this poem which covers a wide field of thought
and speculation, but they may be defended as being essential to
show the world-wide and all-pervading influence of Venus. The
one real and telling fault of *Alma Venus!* as poetry is, ironically
enough, in its structure. To my knowledge, this flaw has been
commented upon only once:

It was really a series of related poems, but these were not always
placed in a position to ensure a continuity of mood or argument. And
the rhymed couplet form did not really suit the theme; there was an
appearance of narrative continuity without the effect. Perhaps if the
different sections of the poem had varied in their form and rhythm
a greater symphonic unity would have been achieved.[7]

V. *Faggot or Cross*

From time to time in a country's literature poets appear who,
if they are to be accepted at all, demand a radical revision of
the dominant conceptions of poetry. When critics do so, it is
quite easy to understand how a general reader may assume the
properties of poetry to be fixed and absolute; a stable world in
the light of which the value of an individual can be judged.
There is a tendency to enter an act of conformity against particular poets where there is difficulty in accommodating them
within the traditionally accepted pattern. This was the fate of
Bernard O'Dowd.

In most critical camps O'Dowd evokes grudging respect for
his honesty, aspiration, and faith; in one quarter however, he
has received what can only be termed "religious" criticism. The
comments of Professors Todd and McAuley have been quoted
in the text of this book. Vincent Buckley, hailed in some academic
halls as the outstanding younger literary critic in Australia, follows the lead of his elders and contributes a statement which
even in its context is nonsensical: "Though politically O'Dowd
was advanced, poetically he was a reactionary, an arthritic, yet
ambitious Shelley chanting of the fabulous destiny of Australian
man, and attempting to show that destiny as part of the wider
glory to which the land itself was destined." [8] Buckley's only
reference is to the earlier poems. Any reader of this commentary
will know that O'Dowd is a more substantial poet than the neo-
Catholic critics credit him with being.

This does not mean he was without flaws; that because he had
a sensitive moral conscience, he was not at times solemn and
pious, that his recondite allusions and esoteric examples were
always fitting to his theme, and that the device of personification,
used to the point of mannerism, did not blur and dilute some
of his images. O'Dowd's faults were many, but in spite of them
he was an effective poet who struck with strength when his aim
was well directed. Personally, I feel there was a touch of the
heroic in a poet who was not afraid to commit himself to opinions and who pursued his way, as he said himself, "Undeterred
by the faggot or cross, uncorrupted by glory or gold."

Henry Green mentions three factors that combined to give
Bernard O'Dowd his reputation. He was the preacher of the
"new democracy" in Australia; he was the intellectual representa-
tive of the nineties; he was a poet of individuality. Political reforms and historical changes have reduced O'Dowd's reputation
to a dependence on the individual quality of his poetry.

In two instances, at least, his achievement was notable. Of its
kind, there is nothing finer in Australian literature than the lyrical
rhapsody *Alma Venus!* and *The Bush* is still, after fifty years,
one of the few outstanding long poems produced in this country.
For the rest there remains an astonishing virtuosity, if not in
form, then of idea; an eager intellectual curiosity and a great
subtlety in expressing views that did not seem before to have
been either subtle or deep.

A tendency to be swamped in sensibility by the press of the
world around him is noticeable in O'Dowd. While he shows an

open attitude to sex, he lacks sensuality. Strong personal emotions are present in all his work, but are overwhelmed by social evils. Throughout his career as a poet he emphasized individual human development yet sought always the communal solution. These contradictions could not be reconciled, as O'Dowd intuitively knew, except by love.

In reaffirming the romantic view of the poet as prophet, C. Day Lewis has beautifully defined the principle of love, as "that reaching out of hands towards the warmth in all things, which is the source and passion of his song. Love is this to him first: but it is more; he apprehends it as a kind of necessity by which all things are bound together and in which, could the whole pattern be seen, their contradictions would appear reconciled." [9]

Notes and References

Chapter One

1. Victor Kennedy and Nettie Palmer, *Bernard O'Dowd* (Melbourne University Press, 1954, p. 26.
2. *Ibid.,* p. 56.
3. *Ibid.,* p. 67.
4. *Ibid.,* pp. 71-2.
5. E. Morris Miller, "Bernard O'Dowd's Early Writing," *Meanjin,* No. 4 (1949), 234.
6. *Lyceum Tutor* (Melbourne, 1888), p. 100.
7. Collected *Poems,* p. 144.
8. "Our Land," Collected *Poems,* p. 258.

Chapter Two

1. Hugh Anderson, *Bernard O'Dowd (1866-1953): An Annotated Bibliography* (Sydney, 1963), p. ix. The note is dated March 1953 and the original ms. is in the University of Texas Library.
2. Kennedy and Palmer, p. 52.
3. *Ibid.,* p. 79.
4. After O'Dowd's death, the author of this book discovered two Sands and McDougall "Australian Rough Diary" in a trunk at the poet's home. All quotations relating to the diaries in this chapter are from transcriptions made in 1956.
5. Kennedy and Palmer, p. 53.
6. *Ibid.,* p. 79.
7. *Ibid.,* p. 53.
8. "O'Dowd to Whitman: Whitman to O'Dowd," *Overland,* No. 23 (1962), 8-18. All subsequent quotations in this chapter are from letters printed in this magazine.

Chapter Three

1. *Bulletin,* May 18, 1895. Final version from Collected *Poems,* p. 67.
2. "Bernard O'Dowd," *Bulletin,* January 6, 1910.
3. A view originating in conversations with O'Dowd during 1951.
4. T. Inglis Moore, *Six Australian Poets,* (Melbourne, 1942), p. 103.
5. *Dawnward?* (Sydney, 1903).

6. Originally owned by Hugh Anderson, now in the Moir Collection of the State Library of Victoria.

7. Ms. in Moir Collection, State Library of Victoria.

8. *Champion*, June 20, 1896.

9. Exodus 3:2. "The burning bush" may be figuratively intense indignation. Quotation is from "Hobb's Digest of Aristotle's Rhetoric," *Aristotle's Poetics*, (Everyman's Library edition No. 901), p. 116.

10. "I kiss the shoulders of the great" is a reference to W. Beckford's *Vathek*, pp. 173-86. (Abbey Classics edition).

11. *Ten Letters* from O'Dowd to A. G. Stephens. Held by the National Library of Australia, Canberra. Dated June 16, 1903.

12. Matthew 13:22. Some varieties of Darnel are poisonous.

13. Shortly before his death, O'Dowd expressed the opinion that *Dawnward?* contained his best work.

14. "Bernard O'Dowd," *Bulletin*, January 6, 1910.

15. "Dawnward?" *Bulletin*, March 10, 1904.

16. Owen Barfield, *Poetic Diction* (London, 1952), p. 91.

17. Rex Warner, *The Cult of Power* (London, 1946), p. 107.

18. "Our Own Social Atmosphere," *Tocsin*, October 16, 1897.

19. Collected *Poems*, p. 70.

20. *Ten Letters*, March 11, 1903. National Library, Canberra.

21. Psalms 106:27.

22. IV, Melbourne, 1887. See also Westermark's *History of Human Marriage*.

23. *Tocsin*, November 4, 1897. The text of the poem appears elsewhere in the same issue.

24. Psalms 106:36-9.

25. "Victorian Illegitimacy and Concubinage," *Tocsin*, December 15, 1898.

26. "Immorality in Victoria," *Tocsin*, Demember 29, 1898.

27. Compare "Wallet of Sigurd shall this swag replace" in "The Bush," *Poems*, p. 188.

Chapter Four

1. Brian Fitzpatrick, *The British Empire in Australia* (Melbourne University Press, 1941), p. 350.

2. See Louise Overacker, *The Australian Party System* (Melbourne, 1952).

3. Quoted in Kennedy and Palmer, p. 110.

4. Quoted in Lloyd Ross, *William Lane and the Australian Labour Movement* (Sydney, n.d.), p. 157.

5. "Fame and Federation," *Tocsin*, October 21, 1897.

6. "Federation and Factories," *Tocsin*, December 2, 1897.

7. *Tocsin*, February 27, 1898.

8. "Federation and the Labor Party," *Tocsin*, March 31, 1898.

9. "Ministries and the Class War," *Tocsin*, December 7, 1899.

10. S. E. Lee, "The Uncollected Poems of Bernard O'Dowd," *Southerly*, No. 2 (1953), 112.

11. James McAuley, *The End of Modernity* (Sydney, 1959), p. 63.

12. Fitzpatrick, pp. 362-3.

13. Lee, p. 113.

14. Many do not make any real sense unless read in conjunction with the analyses of the Bill published serially on May 5, 12, 19, 26 and June 2, 1898.

15. *Federal Convention Debates* (1898), Third Session, II pp. 2506-7.

16. "Federation and Freedom," *Tocsin*, April 14, 1898.

17. *Tocsin*, May 5, 1898.

18. Justices Knox, Isaacs, Rich, and Starke, Engineer's Case (1920), *Commonwealth Law Reports*, XXVIII No. 129 p. 142.

19. "Federation as Proposed," *Tocsin*, February 17, 1898.

20. "Federation," *Tocsin*, April 21, 1898.

21. "Foreboding: A Federation Song," *Tocsin*, June 1, 1898.

22. "Proletaria," *Bulletin*, December 8, 1900. Another version in collected *Poems*, p. 47.

28. *Ten Letters*, March 11, 1903, National Library of Australia.

24. *Tocsin*, July 27, 1899.

25. "The Coming Disaster," *Tocsin*, July 27, 1899.

26. "The *Tocsin* and the Commonwealth," *Tocsin*, July 26, 1900.

27. "Portent," *Tocsin*, January 18, 1900.

Chapter Five

1. *Southerly*, No. 2 (1953), p. 113.

2. *Bulletin*, May 12, 1900.

3. Kennedy and Palmer, p. 121.

4. "That Suppressed Sonnet," *Tocsin*, June 7, 1900.

5. P. Gurrey, *The Appreciation of Poetry*, (London, 1938), p. 23.

6. Matthew 25:2-4.

7. Psalms 137:2.

8. Quotations are from the summary printed in the *Tocsin*, August 7, 1902. The lecture was issued as a pamphlet in the same year.

9. Kennedy and Palmer, p. 115.

10. *Ibid.*, p. 97.

11. First printed in the *Bulletin*, August 29, 1896, but appears in collected *Poems*, pp. 40-2.

12. *Bulletin*, December 8, 1900, and in collected *Poems*, pp. 47-9.

13. Moore, p. 95.

14. This, and the two previous quotations, are from "Young Democracy," *Bulletin*, April 12, 1902, and collected *Poems*, pp. 59-61. The last stanza has been altered to accord with a cutting marked by the poet, now in the possession of the University of Texas Library.

15. Kennedy and Palmer, p. 131.

Chapter Six

1. Ms. in University of Texas Library.
2. March 8, 1902.
3. Quotation is from the *Tocsin*.
4. O'Dowd Newscutting book in the Mitchell Library, pp. 5-6.
5. *Ten Letters*, June 16, 1903. National Library, Canberra.
6. See references in Walter Locke (ed.), *Book of Genesis*, Westminster Commentaries, (London, 1905), p. 108 ff.
7. Daniel 5:24-6.
8. Kennedy and Palmer, p. 101.
9. Dr. Flower, *An Approach to the Psychology of Religion*, (London, 1927).
10. "Closed Road," *Tocsin*, October 2, 1897.
11. "Land Reform," *Tocsin*, January 6, 1898.
12. His return to Christianity is mentioned in a letter containing the Author's Note to *Dawnward?*, held by the Mitchell Library and dated December 21, 1903. "Open the Roads" appeared in the *Westralian Worker*, July 6, 1906. Although it has never been reprinted, O'Dowd did intend adding the poem to any future editions of his collected work.
13. I. Corinthian 15:36-45.
14. *Bulletin*, May 27, 1899.
15. John Bunyan, *The Pilgrim's Progress*, (London, 1942), World Classics edition, pp. 15-16.
16. Quoted in Kennedy and Palmer, p. 126.
17. *Champion*, May 1, 1897.

> Come, Jack, our place is with the ruck
> On the open road today,
> Not with the tepid "footpath sneak"
> Or the wise who stop away.

18. Kennedy and Palmer, p. 132.
19. Moore, p. 91.
20. Reprinted in *Loose Leaves*, (Melbourne, 1910), pp. 83-5.
21. McAuley, pp. 63-4.
22. "Red Page," *Bulletin*, March 10, 1904.
23. "Australian Writers and an English Critic," *Bulletin*, November 30, 1905.

Chapter Seven

1. "Cupid," *Bulletin*, May 12, 1900, and collected *Poems*, pp. 45-7.
2. Collected *Poems*, p. 125.
3. It was not printed until 1905 (*Tocsin*, June 8). Collected *Poems*, pp. 103-5.
4. *A History of Australian Literature*, Vol. I, (Sydney, 1961), p. 505.

5. "Form and Matter in Modern Poetry," *Trident,* August 1908. The manuscript of this lecture is in the University of Texas Library.

6. *Ibid.*

7. Letter dated June 23, 1907. In J. K. Moir Collection, State Library of Victoria.

8. "My Mirandelay," *Bulletin,* October 20, 1910.

9. *Bulletin,* December 15, 1910.

10. "Anti-Mirandelay," *Bulletin,* December 29, 1910.

Chapter Eight

1. Kennedy and Palmer, p. 134.

2. *Ibid.,* p. 189.

3. *Bulletin,* August 27, 1908.

4. *Book Lover,* May 1, 1904.

5. Moore, p. 97.

6. Collected *Poems,* pp. 86-91.

7. "Dominions of the Boundary," *Socialist,* October 19, 1907. Actually the hierarchy begins below the virtues and powers, then come dominations, angels, and archangels.

8. *Loose Leaves,* p. 84.

9. *Australian Literary Essays,* (Sydney, Angus and Robertson, 1957), p. 40, and *Six Australian Poets,* p. 106.

10. II, p. 504.

11. "The Abiding Gods," collected *Poems,* pp. 110-11.

12. "Hermes," collected *Poems,* pp. 131-6.

13. I. Samuel 28:7-10.

14. Collected *Poems,* p. 112.

15. "Red Page," *Bulletin,* November 21, 1907.

16. "Mystic," collected *Poems,* p. 111.

17. Collected *Poems,* pp. 137-8.

18. Collected *Poems,* pp. 141-5.

Chapter Nine

1. S. E. Lee, p. 120.

2. *Poetry Militant,* in a revised form, prefaces collected *Poems,* pp. 3-32.

3. St. John 1:23.

4. Moore, p. 86.

5. F. M. Todd, "The Poetry of Bernard O'Dowd," *Meanjin,* No. 1 (1955), 92.

6. "Delmar Fenton," "The Spiritual Militant," *This World and the Next,* December 14, 1895.

7. "What I said in 1909 I say today. I still stand by *Poetry Militant.*" Quoted by Ian Mair, "Laws and Songs: Bernard O'Dowd," *Weekend Review,* November 3, 1950.

8. "Wordsworth," *Socialist*, September 14, 1907.
9. "Dreamers and Doers," *Spectator* (Melbourne), June 24, 1942. Abridged report only.
10. "Poetry Militant," *Bulletin*, June 17, 1909.
11. *Spectator*, October 20, 1943. Abridged report only.
12. Moore, p. 86.
13. Green, I, p. 503.
14. Todd, *op. cit.*
15. Frederick T. Macartney, *Australian Literary Essays*, (Sydney, 1957), p. 37.
16. A. A. Phillips (ed.), *Bernard O'Dowd*, (Sydney, 1963), Australian Poets Series, p. viii.
17. *Ibid.*, p. ix.
18. *Ibid.*, p. xi.
19. Macartney, p. 32.
20. Walter Murdoch and others, "Tribute to the Memory of Bernard O'Dowd," *Meanjin*, No. 4 (1953), p. 419.
21. Kennedy and Palmer, p. 3.
22. *Ibid.*, p. 187.

Chapter Ten

1. Moore, p. 92.
2. Kennedy and Palmer, p. 188.
3. "Bernard O'Dowd," *Bulletin*, January 6, 1910.
4. Moore, p. 91.
5. Collected *Poems*, p. 159.
6. Macartney, pp. 141-2.
7. Todd, p. 95.
8. Phillips, p. xi.
9. "Is Australia a Democracy?" *Spectator* (Melbourne), August 30, 1944. Abridged report only.
10. Collected *Poems*, p. 166.
11. Kennedy and Palmer, p. 188.
12. Collected *Poems*, p. 167.
13. "Literature in Australia," *Corroboree* (July 1922), pp. 2-5, continued in (August 1922), pp. 1-4. Abridged report only.
14. Collected *Poems*, pp. 183-4.
15. "Right Side Up," *Advance Australia* (March 1897).
16. Collected *Poems*, p. 168.
17. "A Motto for Australia," *Socialist*, September 7, 1907.

Chapter Eleven

1. "The Bush," *Bulletin*, January 16, 1913.
2. Moore, p. 92.
3. Macartney, p. 45.

4. F. T. Macartney, "The Poetry of Bernard O'Dowd," *Meanjin,* No. 2 (1949), p. 81.
5. Kennedy and Palmer, p. 150.
6. "Literature in Australia," *Corroboree* (August 1922).
7. "Dream Times," *Advance Australia* (June 1897).
8. "The Mission of the Syllabus," *Advance Australia* (March 1897).
9. Quotations in this paragraph are from separate articles by A. R. Chisholm; "The Bush: A Landmark," *Southerly,* No. 2 (1953), pp. 90-92, and "Bernard O'Dowd," *Meanjin,* No. 1 (1954), pp. 136-7.
10. *Southerly,* No. 2 (1953), p. 91.
11. Matthew 7:7-8.
12. Deuteronomy 32:13.
13. "Morgana Mine and Other Realities," *Fantasies* (included in the second and subsequent edition of the collected *Poems*).
14. Kennedy and Palmer, p. 153.

Chapter Twelve

1. David M. Wright, "Lust and Love," *Bulletin,* December 29, 1921.
2. Quoted by Kennedy and Palmer, p. 162.
3. "Editorial Notes," *Birth* (February 1922).
4. Quoted by Kennedy and Palmer, p. 191. Letter dated March 12, 1922.
5. Macartney, p. 42. Letter dated October 8, 1913.
6. Kennedy and Palmer, p. 163.
7. *Ibid.,* p. 161.
8. Vincent Buckley, *Essays in Poetry* mainly Australian (Melbourne University Press, 1957), p. 11.
9. C. Day Lewis, *The Poetic Image* (London, 1947).

Selected Bibliography

PRIMARY SOURCES

Poetry

DAWNWARD? Sydney, The Bulletin Newspaper Co., 1903. Another edition: Melbourne, 1909, pp. 47.

THE SILENT LAND *and other verses*. Melbourne, T. C. Lothian, 1906. Another edition: Melbourne, 1909, pp. 63.

DOMINIONS OF THE BOUNDARY. Melbourne, T. C. Lothian, 1907, pp. 65.

THE SEVEN DEADLY SINS: *A Series of sonnets and other verses*. Melbourne, T. C. Lothian, 1909, pp. 53.

POEMS. Melbourne, T. C. Lothian, 1910, pp. 92.

THE BUSH. Melbourne, T. C. Lothian, 1912, pp. 69.

ALMA VENUS! *and other verses*. Melbourne, Lothian Book Publishing Co., 1921, pp. 27.

THE POEMS OF BERNARD O'DOWD. *Collected Edition*. Melbourne, Lothian Publishing Co., 1941, pp. 286. Reprinted 1943 and 1944. Introduction by Walter Murdoch.

BERNARD O'DOWD. Sydney, Angus and Robertson, 1963, pp. 62. "Australian Poets" series. Selection and Introduction by A. A. Phillips.

Prose

DEMOCRACY AND CONSCIENCE. Melbourne, "The Tocsin" Office, 1902, pp. 23.

POETRY MILITANT: *An Australian plea for the poetry of purpose*. Melbourne, T. C. Lothian, 1909, pp. 54.

FANTASIES. Melbourne, Lothian Publishing Co., 1942, pp. 22.

SECONDARY SOURCES

Bibliography

ANDERSON, HUGH. *Bernard O'Dowd* (1866-1953): An Annotated bibliography. Sydney, Wentworth Books, 1963, pp. 52. Processed. "Studies in Australian Bibliography," No. 12. Contains a Preliminary Note by Bernard O'Dowd, written in March 1953; a complete listing of poetry and prose publications, edited books and prefaces; poetry and prose contributions to periodicals and newspapers; lectures existing in manuscript; law books; it also lists and annotates general criticisms, and articles on O'Dowd printed since 1947.

————. "A List of Uncollected Poems," *Southerly*, XIV, No. 2 (1953), 125. "O'Dowd in Disguise," *Southerly*, XIV, No. 2 (1953), 125. A brief comment on nom de plumes used by O'Dowd and their meaning.

CHAPLIN, HARRY. "Early Editions of Bernard O'Dowd," *Biblionews* (March, 1950). Describes the *Lyceum Tutor* (1888) and variant editions of *Dawnward?* (1903).

MACARTNEY, FREDERICK T. (ed.) *Australian Literature*. Sydney, Angus and Robertson, 1956, pp. 361-63. Contains a book list and a concise account of the main poems.

MILLER, E. MORRIS. *Australian Literature*. Melbourne University Press, 2 vol., 1940, various pages. Provides detailed book lists and a succinct appraisal of O'Dowd's poetry and philosophy.

STEPHENS, A. G. "The Most Conscientious," *Bookfellow* (June 1914). Stephens discusses the three changes made during the printing of *Dawnward?*: two copies appeared with an "Author's Note"; 50 copies with the poem "May Day" but omitting both the "Author's Note" and a "Personal Note" (by A. G. Stephens); and 50 copies for subscribers that included the "Personal Note" and omitted the "Author's Note" and "May Day."

Biography

KENNEDY, VICTOR and NETTIE PALMER. *Bernard O'Dowd*. Melbourne University Press, 1954, p. 194. The only biography of the poet yet available. Begun in 1950 by Victor Kennedy and completed after his death by Nettie Palmer, the book "is in no sense a complete biography" and was written with the modest aim of "giving a coherent account of the poet's origins and upbringing, of venturing some appraisement of his work, of suggesting the sort of influences that affected him and the way he, in turn, has left his mark through his poetry and personal convictions on the Australia of his time." It is also, in a sense, an "official" biography as the poet read and approved its contents before publication, and, indeed, supplied most of the biographical detail. There are several important errors of fact and an extreme reticence concerning Mrs. O'Dowd and Mrs. Marie Pitt.

BAKER, KATE. "Bernard Patrick O'Dowd," *Southerly*, XIV, No. 2 (1953), 81-3. A quite vivid, though apparently erroneous story of O'Dowd conducting his Sunday study classes. Corrected by Frederick T. Macartney in "A Footnote to Bernard O'Dowd," *Meanjin*, XIV, No. 1 (Autumn 1955), 142-43.

BRADY, EDWIN J. "Bernard O'Dowd," *All About Books* (July 1929). A general survey of the poetry and a brief biography which is important for its reference to the reasons for which O'Dowd resigned as *Tocsin* joint-editor.

COBBETT, S. "Bernard O'Dowd, Our National Poet," *Herald* (Melbourne), (July 19, 1941). Gives a brief review of O'Dowd's life as exemplified by his publications. Most emphasis is placed on the political aspects of the subject matter of *Dawnward?*

FAY, J. "Bernard O'Dowd and the War," *Socialist* (October 23, 1914). A letter attacking O'Dowd over an alleged change of attitude to the War.

FOSTER, A. W. "Bernard O'Dowd, Rationalist," *Meanjin*, XIV, No. 1 (Autumn 1955), 143. Mr. Justice Foster points out that the obituaries of O'Dowd neglect to mention his work as an editor of the *Tocsin* and his life as "a prominent and vigorous rationalist."

HOLBURN, MUIR. "Poet of Force and Courage," *Book News* (May, 1947). The collected edition of *Poems* does not "give any idea of the immense influence he exercised in the early years of the Commonwealth [of Australia] nor of the part he played in shaping and enriching the ideas of his day." O'Dowd's primary concern was with people and their genuine interests.

MAIR, IAN. "Laws and Songs: Bernard O'Dowd," *Week-End Review* (November 3, 1950). Mair describes O'Dowd at the age of eighty-four years, his opinions on writing in Australia, something of his life, and his house at Northcote.

"Monsieur Parapluie," *Bookfellow* (July 1920). A humorous anecdote of O'Dowd's visit to Sydney by Messageries Maritime Service; the amazement and perplexity of the French sailors at the poet's devotion to his umbrella.

MURDOCH, WALTER, *and others*. "Tributes to the Memory of Bernard O'Dowd," *Meanjin*, XII, No. 4 (Summer 1953), 407-19. Various reminiscences of O'Dowd at different points in his life by Walter Murdoch, Mary Gilmore, Frederick T. Macartney, Nettie Palmer, E. Morris Miller, Tom Inglis Moore, and Katharine Susannah Prichard.

"O'Dowd to Whitman, Whitman to O'Dowd," *Overland*, No. 23 (Autumn 1962) 8-18. First publication in Australia of the total correspondence between the two poets, and first publication of a letter from Whitman (dated March 15, 1891). With this exception, the letters were printed in *Walt Whitman's Review* (June 1961), together with an article by A. L. McLeod on "Walt Whitman in Australia."

"Personal Items," *Bulletin* (January 9, 1913). Comments on O'Dowd as Chairman of the Fibrous Plasterer's Wages Board with his possible judgment in verse. A news report of the Board's deliberations appeared in the *Herald* (Melbourne), October 29, 1913.

STEPHENS, A. G. "The Month," *Bookfellow* (November 1912). O'Dowd is taken to task over his statements on authors' returns. His royalties in 1911 on five books of verse were £ 1.17s.

General Criticism

"Australian Writers and an English Critic," *Bulletin*, (November 30, 1905). Prints the comments of Australian authors represented in *A Southern Garland* on a review, "Crabbed Age and Youth," in the *Academy* (London), September 9, 1905. O'Dowd vigorously defends the verses in *Dawnward?* and makes several valuable points regarding the judgement of verse quality.

CHISHOLM, A. R. "The Bush: A Landmark," *Southerly*, XIV, No. 2 (1953), 90-93. This poem is a milestone in the history of poetry in Australia. Until 1912 O'Dowd's poetry "lacked an anthropological background." *The Bush* is a special statement of the Eternal Recurrence doctrine.

————. "Bernard O'Dowd," *Meanjin*, XIII, No. 1 (Autumn 1954), 136-37. There is an "obvious influence of Nietzsche" on O'Dowd's poetry. O'Dowd had "an essentially metaphysical imagination" and his writing tended towards incantation; "it was personal magic and a true song."

EWERS, JOHN K. *Creative Writing in Australia*. Melbourne, Georgian House, 1962, pp. 71-5, 77, and various pages. Finds in O'Dowd's Poetry three "driving forces: a strong humanitarianism, a sense of spiritual and mystical values, and a clamant Australianism," and considers each in relation to particular poems.

GRATTAN, C. H. *Australian Literature*. University of Washington Book Store, 1929, pp. 29-30. An informed American observer's opinion of O'Dowd's standing as an Australian poet, especially in his social role.

GREEN, HENRY M. *An Outline of Australian Literature*. Sydney, Whitcombe and Tombs, 1930, pp. 164-69, and various pages. Sketches briefly the poet's life, but most space is devoted to comment on the images found in the booklets of verse.

————. *Fourteen Minutes*. Sydney, Angus and Robertson, 1944, pp. 69-76. To the extent O'Dowd is a poet, "he is a poet in spite of himself," but nevertheless, "one of the most remarkable personalities in Australian literature." Remarks on a poetic change in middle life when "the plant yielded flower and fruit together."

————. *A History of Australian Literature*. Sydney, Angus and Robertson, 2 vol., 1961, I, 463-64, 504-9, and various pages. A full, and generally fair, account of the poetry; comparisons with Henry Lawson and Christopher Brennan are made. The view expressed by Green in *A History* has not greatly changed since 1930 and later critical articles have not been referred to.

MACARTNEY, FREDERICK T. "Bernard O'Dowd," *Australian Literary Essays*. Sydney, Angus and Robertson, 1957, pp. 32-46. An informative personal view of O'Dowd's poetry, together with interesting sidelights on the poet's life.

MOORE, TOM INGLIS. *Six Australian Poets.* Melbourne, Robertson and Mullens, 1942, pp. 85-109. A critical, detailed analysis of all aspects of O'Dowd's poetry that has not been surpassed by any other critic.

LEE, S. E. "The Uncollected Poems of Bernard O'Dowd," *Southerly,* XIV, No. 2 (1953), 110-24. A useful survey of certain verses from the *Tocsin* and a few from the *Bulletin* that have not been reprinted.

MACARTNEY, FREDERICK T. "The Poetry of Bernard O'Dowd," *Meanjin,* VIII, No. 2 (Winter 1949), 81-91. Begins with O'Dowd reading his Presidential address to the Literature Society in 1909, and is followed by notes of personal associations in various societies. The article then advances to a very fair and balanced review of the poetry.

MILLER, E. MORRIS. "Bernard O'Dowd's Early Writings," *Meanjin,* VIII, No. 4 (Summer 1949), 233-39. The study of the contributions of O'Dowd to the *Lyceum Tutor* (1888) indicates that the printed work of this writer must be dated, not from *Dawnward?,* but fifteen years earlier. Themes of verse in the *Tutor* persisted in the later poetry. Miller's article is particularly valuable for its discussion of O'Dowd's philosophical development.

————. "O'Dowd's *The Bush:* An Exposition," *Diogenes* (University of Tasmania), No. 3 (1957). Delivered in Adelaide in 1955 as one of the Commonwealth Literary Fund Lectures for that year, this lecture is possibly the most searching examination of the poetic and philosophical basis of O'Dowd's outstanding poem.

STEWART, DOUGLAS. "A Man with a Vision," *Bulletin* (January 28, 1942). This is a thoughtful, important, and sympathetic view of O'Dowd as an Australian poet. He has come to a "second crop," to recognition as Australia's national poet, because he is needed. But besides the patriotic need there is a poetic need.

TODD, F. M. "The Poetry of Bernard O'Dowd," *Meanjin,* XIV, No. 1 (Autumn 1955), 91-7. Although Bernard O'Dowd made a considerable contribution to the establishment of Australian literature, his preconception as to the nature of poetry and his lack of the "poet's sense of reality" prevented him being a better poet. His achievement was a consequence of his patriotism and personality and "almost unrelated to the artistic merit of his work." The dignity he strove for was often spurious and his major mannerisms of political rhetoric, windy generalisation and topsy-turvy personification, indicate his insensitivity. Yet behind all these faults, Todd believes there was a real poet who was successful in some of the sonnets.

Index

Adams, Francis, 24
Advance Australia, 127n
Anthology of Australian Verse, An, 67
Appreciation of Poetry, The, 124n
Approach to the Psychology of Religion, An, 125n
Aristotle's Poetics, 123n
Australian Church Debating Society, 24
Australian Literary Essays, 127n
Australian Party System, The, 123n
Australian Race, The, 34

Baere, Harry de, *see* de Baere, Harry
Ballarat, 16
Beaufort, 15, 16, 107, 108
Berkeley, George (1685-1753), 93, 94
Birth, 128n
Blake, William, 77
British Empire in Australia, The, 123n
Buckley, Vincent, 120
Bulletin, 30, 47, 55, 56, 63, 64, 70-71, 72, 75, 79, 84, 99, 104
Bury, Thomas, 17, 23, 27

Campbell, Wilfred, 74
Carlyle, Thomas (1795-1881), 93
Castieau, Jack, 38
Challenger (ship), 48
Champion, 125n
Chisholm, A.R., 101-102
Commonwealth Law Reports, 124n
Corbett, Hugh, 38

Corroboree, 127n
Courier (Ballarat), 17
Cult of Power, The, 123n
Curr, E.M., 34

Daley, Victor, 39
de Baere, Harry, 15, 17
Deakin, Alfred, 42
Decline and Fall of the Roman Empire, 56

Ellis, A.D., 113
End of Modernity, The, 124n
Essays in Poetry, 128n
Evening Post (Ballarat), 16
Emerson, Ralph Waldo, 73, 76

Fall of the Roman Empire, 59-60
Findley, E., 39
Free Thought, 17, 20-21
Fryer family, 21, 24
Fryer, Ada, 27
Fryer, Evangeline, 21, 66-67, 69-70

Gordon, Adam Lindsay, 20
Green, Henry M., 77, 86, 120

Harbinger of Light, 17
Hartigan, James, 27
Higinbotham, George, 30
Higgins, Henry Bournes, 100
History of Australian Literature, A, 125n
History of Human Marriage, The, 123n
Howarth, R.G., 12
Hume, David (1711-1776), 93, 94

Jephcott, Sydney, 23, 66

135

Kant, Immanuel, 92-94
Kennedy, Victor, and Palmer, Nettie, 88-89, 100, 118, 119
Lane, William, 40
Leaves of Grass, 25-26
Lee, S.E., 47
Lewis, Cecil Day, 121
Liberator, 17
Lindsay, Lionel, 39
Loose Leaves, 125n, 126n
Lyceum, Melbourne, 20
Lyceum Leader, 20
Lyceum Tutor, 21

Macartney, Frederick T., 77, 86, 88, 91-92, 100, 102, 117
Meanjin, 122n, 126n, 127n, 128n
Miller, E. Morris, 2-22
Miller, Minnie, 17
Moir Collection (State Library of Victoria), 123n, 126n
Moore, T. Inglis, 29, 64, 76, 77, 82, 86, 95, 99
Murdoch, Walter, 64, 77, 87, 112
McAuley, James, 42, 64, 120
McKay, H.C., 71-72

National Library of Australia (Canberra), 123n, 124n
Neilson, Shaw, 84
Northcote (Melbourne), 69

O'Dowd, Amergin (son), 67
O'Dowd, Auster (son), 67
O'Dowd, Bernard Patrick:
    appearance, 15, 27; children, 66-67; democracy, views on, 50-51, 53; diary, 1889, 25; employment, 15, 16, 28; federation, views on, 40ff; Labor Party, and, 38, 40, 41; land reform, views on, 59; law studies, 19; literary societies, and, 25; love affairs, 18, 66ff; marriage, 66; Melbourne in 1886, 15, 19; parents, 15, 16; political journalism, 39-40, 59; pseudonyms, 17, 39; reading, 15; religion, 15, 16-17, 18, 62, 63; schooling,

15, 16; socialism, 40; verse, early, 16, 17-18; verse technique, 65, 90-92; Whitman, letters to, 26-28

WRITINGS OF:

Alma Venus! 111-119
"Athena", 80-81
"Auster Rampant!" 96-97
"Australia", 47, 148-50
"Australia Mavoureen", 97-98
"Avarice", 91
"Bacchus", 22, 81
"Bottom Dog Brigade, The", 95-96
Bush, The, 15, 72, 99-110
"Campfires of the Lost, The", 53
"Compromise", 29-31
"Cow, The", 94
"Cupid", 67, 114
"Dawnward?" 44-45, 55-59
Dawnward? 29, 32-33, 44, 47, 52, 54, 63, 64, 65, 74, 77
"Democracy and Conscience" (lecture), 50, 53, 55
Dominions of the Boundary, 67, 76, 77-81, 111
"Early Days of Victoria, The" (lecture), 20
"Earth", 76
"Envy", 91
"Fallow", 74
"False Accusations", 16
Fantasies, 128n
"Fas", 74
"Federal Plot, The", 42-43
"Foreboding", 43-44, 45
"Give me a God", 19
"Gluttony", 91
"Gods, The", 76
"Goodbye Ben!" 61
"Hark now the joy bells . . .", 17
"Heracleitic", 79
"Hermes", 78
"Hoist the Flag", 22

"I loved you long, I loved you well . . .", 18

"Isis", 76

"Juno", 76, 77, 114

"Land of the Terrible Rite, The", 34-37

"Love and Sacrifice", 68-69

"Love's Substitute", 67

"Lust", 111

"Marching on to Hell", 19

"May Day", 63

"Mirandelay", 70-72

"Mnemosyne", 77

"My Own Dear Love", 16

"New Tertullian, A", 22

"O Leave Her", 16

"Ode to Sydney", 72

"One summer morn with sketching book . . .", 18

"Open the Roads", 60-62

"Our Duty", 68

"Poet, The", 95

Poetry Militant, 76, 82-89, 94, 114

"Portent", 45-46

"Practical Christianity" (lecture), 20

"Pride", 90-91

"Proletaria", 43, 44, 52

"Quail", 74

"Seed Time, The", 34-37

Seven Deadly Sins, The, 90-98, 111

Silent Land, The, 73-77, 94

"Sirens", 76

"Sloth", 91

"Solitude", 16

"Song of Hate", 31-32

"Stealthy Squadrons of the Foe, The", 45

"Threshold Murmurs", 76

"To All Eternity", 16

"To Immanuel Kant", 92-94

"Venus Genetrix", 67, 111

"Winds", 77

"Young Democracy", 53

O'Dowd, Mrs. B., *see* Fryer, Evangeline

O'Dowd, Montaigne (son), 66

O'Dowd, Rudel (son), 67

O'Dowd, Vondel (son), 67

Overland, 122n

Palmer, Nettie, 11, 66, 89, 90, 91, 94; *see also* Kennedy, Victor

Phillips, Arthur A., 86, 87, 88

Pilgrim's Progress, The, 125n

Pitt, Marie, 69, 70, 104

Pleasant Sunday Afternoon (Wesley Church), 83-84

Poe, Edgar Allan, 77

Poetic Diction, 123n

Poetic Image, The, 128n

Prendergast, George, 38

Prichard, Katharine S., 88

Sandringham (Vic.), 24

Shah Nameh, 31-32, 39

Shakespeare, William, 24, 53

Socialist (Melb.), 126n, 127n

Southerly, 124n, 128n

Southern Garland, A, 19-20, 64

Spectator (Melb.), 127n

Spencer, Herbert, 25

Stephens, A.G., 19, 31, 44, 56, 63, 105, 112

Tempest, The, 48

This World and the Next, 126n

Tocsin, 34, 36, 37, 38ff, 58, 60

Todd, F.M., 83, 86, 120

"Tom Touchstone" *see* Bury, Thomas

Trident, 126n

Tunnecliffe, Thomas, 42

"Under the Lindens", 30

University of Texas, Library, 122n, 124n, 125n

Vathek, 123n

Weekend Review, 126n

Westralian Worker, 125n

Whitman, Walt, 23-28, 103

William Lane and the Australian   Wordsworth, William, 84
    Labour Movement, 123n   Wright, David McKee, 112, 113-
Woods, Frederick, 15, 17, 20, 24,   114
    27